AF472446

Our First Encore

With a Foreward by Gaylene Lesser

AuthorHouse™ UK Ltd.
500 Avebury Boulevard
Central Milton Keynes, MK9 2BE
www.authorhouse.co.uk
Phone: 08001974150

First published by AuthorHouse 3/9/2011

ISBN: 978-1-4490-8642-8 (sc)

Foreword

Lulu Gee and Dan Lake have given me the honour of writing this introduction to their latest joint production of this book of poems. I say this is an honour because I am not one who has been a writer of poetry for very long and will be a lifelong learner of the joy and intricacies of expressing my own thoughts.

As a school teacher for 35 years I taught poetry writing to my students, but to find poems that would spark their muse was, believe it or not, quite difficult. It was a genre that was somewhat neglected and poems for children are few and far between today and not so actively encouraged in many schools.

Children love to hear, read and write in rhyme. It appeals to their sense of an ordered world and can almost sound like a song. I found they would love to and easily learn verse in rhyme, one of their favourites being the Australian poet, 'Banjo Paterson'. They loved dramatising these rhyming poems with a story and we had much fun during these times.

This brings me to the poetry of Lulu and Dan, whom I met on an interactive poetry site, where their poems very quickly became my favourites to read. Our friendship grew and their poetry has become an integral part of my daily dose of reading!

Both Lulu and Dan write in such flawless rhyme that each poem is such a pleasure to read, no matter the subject. Lulu has the precious ability to write rhyme that is particularly suited to the child in us all and every piece will bring some sense of joy to your heart. Her children's' poetry has a special place in my heart.

Dan writes on a myriad of subjects and his rhyme makes you want to read so many different topics that he is so adept at. He has thoughts that are deep and profound and his reality is often very thought provoking, yet he has the sensibilities of a true gentleman.

The writings of both Lulu and Dan have a place in everyone's life, from childhood to adulthood and are a fine learning tool on love, life and fantasy, from their combined life experience.

I thank them both most sincerely for this honour and am humbled by their request.

Gaylene Lesser
October 2010

The Heart Knows What The Eye Can't See

Remember dark and light so fills the world
that both will battle for the spirit's sense.
The seeing eye will catch all that is hurled,
if not curtailed is left without defence.

So eye must question heart for where truth lies,
for heart has depth of wisdom eye can't know.
That judgement then will sift through all disguise
to leave the way as white as purest snow.

So future path is clear and finely keyed
to follow dreams that lead a life in light.
Then truth can race as swift as mighty steed,
for heart has known the depth of darkest night.

So follow mighty heart your destiny
and eye will know sincere serenity.

Gaylene Lesser

Contents

The Golden Orb

Within the golden orb I've dried,
alone, I missed my cue.
The audience is terse, they chide,
I've cocked up my debut.
An awful thought of déjà vu
imbues my mind with dread,
I should have danced a pas de deaux
but stand alone instead.
The moment that I've come to fear,
(I wanted to eschew,)
my muse has simply left my dear!
I don't know what to do.
How best to salvage this review
I'm at an awkward age,
I'd rather walk to Timbuktu
than dry up on this stage…

Dan Lake

Heads and Hearts

Should my head rule my heart, it's often said
Or my heart rule my head, this is the ruse,
Should my head rule my heart, (I'll never wed)
Or my heart rule my head, (I do confuse.)
I tarry on this question, I might lose
But I don't want to seem I'm easy led,
I have no need to go and sing the blues,
But have the need to want to share my bed.

Naïve and fazed, I'm also poorly read
'If only I could walk in Hardy's shoes,'
Would then I turn the ladies heads instead,
Would words ensure that love alone ensues.
Enough, enough I know not what to choose,
I can't control these thoughts here in my head,
'My head, my heart, I think I'll take a snooze'
And hope, awakening, these thoughts have fled.

I've stretched and yawned when rising from my bed
And remember what my father often said
'There's more and more again fish in the sea,'
So when I fish, 'there'll be one left for me.'

Dan Lake

I'll Look Around

There is a garden somewhere waits for me,
With twisty vines and trees extraordinaire,
Where on a summer's day
When dreams are far away,
I'll look around and know that you are there.

A garden facing out towards the sea,
Where I can sit with sunlight in my hair
And when the seagulls call
To warn me of a squall,
I'll look around and know that you are there.

There is a cottage by a lonely beach,
With rocks where I can clamber without care,
When kissing waves embrace
A rainbow giving chase,
I'll look around and know that you are there.

A cottage with a rose around the door,
Where peonies will bloom most everywhere
And when I hear your feet
On stairs echoing sweet,
I'll look around and know that you are there.

There is a garden gate to lead me to,
A door that opens to a cottage where,
My happiness will lie
Until the day I die,
I'll look around and know that you are there.

Lulu Gee

Those Were the Days (Quatern)

Those were the days when life was fine
When boys smiled sweetly at her door,
She often thought of love, divine,
Her sweetheart, her dear paramour.

She'd chosen him, so long ago;
Those were the days when life was fine,
Her blue eyed boy, her young Franco
With arms so strong and lips like wine.

Those things taboo on which they'd dine,
That fruit of life tasted so sweet,
Those were the days when life was fine,
Her smile, his love, life was complete.

A tear appeared within her eye,
Her body weary, bent by time,
She felt the burden of her sigh;
Those were the days when life was fine…

Dan Lake

Autumn Colours

Oh! My heart's in Cumbria,
That for so long I've missed,
The blue grey hills and valleys
As flaming Autumn's kissed.
For not since young I've seen it
Beneath an Autumn sky,
When at dawn in soft grey mist
I watched the clouds race by.

The lakes 'neath mountain summits
Are deepest peacock green,
With trees aflamed with Autumn,
The like you've never seen!
For colours rich in texture
Are painting gold the hills
And heathers bathe in purples,
Ahead of winter chills.

While in the amber sunshine
By silver tarns that flow,
The low-land sheep are grazing
Where Autumn breezes blow
And o'er beyond in Keswick,
You'll see the ospreys there,
Among the blue of shadows
Where sights of them are rare.

And should you walk yet higher
To climb the tallest peak,
There's snow as white as crystal
Where clouds will brush your cheek.
My heart so loves this landscape
That Autumn's long desired,
The lakes and fells and mountains,
Where poets are inspired.

The bronze and gold this season
Will nestle on the brink,
Of shores beside pearl waters,
Where trout and salmon slink.
Oh! My heart's in Cumbria,
That for so long I've missed
But hope prevails I may return
To keep an Autumn tryst.

Lulu Gee

The Prisoner

Imprisoned here for year on year
Beneath the earth's shadows,
With walls so thick she feels panic
Held hostage by psychos.

Her silent cries with painful sighs
Are never heard above
The darkened cell, the living hell
With neither care nor love.

She is abused by those amused
Who come to her each night,
As time stands still without freewill
From her appalling plight.

Her loved ones weak still yearly seek
A daughter lost at nine,
But now she's grown, she won't be known
As little Caroline!

Lulu Gee

I Fingered It

I fingered it and thumbed it,
I stroked it and I strummed it,
I pushed inside to inspect every space,
Its beauty made me kiss it
And I swore that I should miss it,
If I ne're again I felt its warm embrace.

I played with it, beguiled with it,
I sat and simply smiled at it,
I knew our recreation would go far,
I bless the day I clocked it,
When I held it there and rocked it,
That perfect day I got my first guitar.

Well what did you expect…a motor car?

Dan Lake

One Day

One day when I'm out riding and with friends perhaps confiding,
is that the day my love will come for me?
When I'm feeling kinda lonesome, forlorn or on my ownsome,
I'll see him looking handsome and carefree.

Or perhaps when I'm snowballing and everything's enthralling,
as snowflakes fall so even, crisp and sweet.
When swans fly proudly overhead going to their nesting bed,
I'll see him with snowdrops around his feet.

Perhaps when I'm star gazing at the heavens so amazing,
as I laze beneath the willow in twilight.
When the moon is drifting high kissing the purple of the sky,
I'll hear his voice call softly in the night.

It could be early morning with a saffron sun adorning,
in springtime, restless summer or the fall.
Or when I read my latest book over by the babbling brook,
maybe I'll see him standing there so tall.

Or as I lie daydreaming with my sleepy head a scheming,
within my pretty garden in mid June.
Or alone sipping cocoa I'll hear his footstep and I'll know,
At last, he's here and I'm over the moon.

Lulu Gee

Wonderment of Youth

Wistful whiles of innocence
Laid bare upon the sand,
Those dreams of perpetuity
Aspiring dreams so planned.
Washed away so long ago
By seas of scornful truth.
Those dreams of gold were mine to hold,
In wonderment of youth.

Dan Lake

Lace Curtains

From my window I can see
O'er the Lammas land,
To the park in Godalming
With our new bandstand,
Curved and rounded like the moon,
Laughing with delight,
Where musicians play in tune
On a summer's night.

Geese and water meadow birds
Rest upon the bank,
Peaceful at the river's edge,
Where the swans outrank.
Ancient willows gently sway
Softly in the breeze,
Ruffling new, downy feathers,
Making children sneeze.

Beyond the far horizon,
Charterhouse I see,
I think it must be sports day
With its grand marquee
Glistening like a diamond
High upon Furze hill,
And towers over school life
And the old flour mill.

More rapid is the river,
Rushing past my door,
A storm channel, it quivers,
Out pouring a roar.
While tall bamboos are clicking,
Loud and proud and slim,
Advising the young ducklings,
Being taught to swim.

There above the clock tower,
Far beyond the park,
Sunlight pours her liquid gold
On a lone skylark.
All peeked through a veil of lace,
Draped with satin ties,
Oh! What busy goings on
Is spread before my eyes.

Lulu Gee

Her Stolen World

Staring into dormant space she thinks about that last embrace,
when she kissed her gentle man goodbye.
Another tear runs to her chin then dripping on her naked skin
it joins the stream that trickles down her thigh.

Imagining he's with her still she tries to conjure up the thrill
and kissed her hands, as she would kiss his face,
She sees his tender loving eyes, then slowly as the vision dies
her mind drifts to a time, another place.

She holds him, sleeping in her arms, he's loved her using all his charms,
(he's not the man that he once used to be.)
Like her he's worn from life's advance, but still she sees his blue eyes dance,
He's everything she wants, her potpourri.

She only has him for a while, to hold his arm, to see him smile,
precious moments, jewels for her to reap,
She sighs and dreams of moments when, they'll be together once again,
then languishing she hugs herself to sleep.

To sleep and then perchance to dream, to worlds beyond her mortal scheme,
Her stolen world, where he'll be hers to keep.

Dan Lake

The Men from Nowhere

He came from nowhere, out of sight
With eyes intent on harm,
She screamed and putting up a fight
He shook her to be calm.
Then roughly forced her to the ground,
While others quickly tightly bound,
  To keep her still
  To keep her still
And silence her with scarves that wound.

Her eyes with terror stared at stars
And at the moon now dim,
And was that smell of stale cigars
On shirts of blue denim.
They laughed and ridiculed each thrust
With sickening enraging lust,
  Their mocking scorn
  Their mocking scorn
Made her repulsive with disgust.

Her body, they rolled to and fro
Upon the ground so cold,
And someone in a red bandeau
Had her in stranglehold.
And all the while they drank whisky,
While getting evermore frisky,
  With no escape
  With no escape
From their merciless savagery.

And then their laughter was no more
As silence filled the air,
With eyes that wept and broken jaw
And body bruised and bare.
A broken doll near death, in pain,
Impregnated by men, insane,
  Then left to die
  Then left to die
Another victim of cocaine!

She lay all night close to death's door,
Until a passer-by,
Saw her beneath the prickly haw
And trembled with a sigh.
What animals could do this deed?
To leave her here to weep and bleed
  And die in pain
  And die in pain
Beside a field of gold rapeseed.

Lulu Gee

Luscious Lulu (a rugby poem)

She was luscious Lulu Lanker
Succulent young rugby flanker,
Game plan stickler, mistake spanker,
Built to play for hours.

She was a female team tight head hitter,
Dangerous, a fearful critter,
Fighting to the end, no quitter
(Severe in the showers.)

Often games were torn asunder,
Blown apart by Lulu's thunder,
Men would cow to our girls wonder,
You could hear their screams.

She punished those for indecision,
Treating them with curt derision,
In the shower, (full incision,)
Ride them to extremes.

Bent and worn out they'd escape her,
Hardly lighting her touch paper,
None could please her, none could sate her,
Quell her huge desire.

Then one day a new team player
Huge Henry the perfect stayer,
Adonis, a woman slayer,
Joined, and lit her fire.

In the shower he was tumbled,
Into Lulu he soon rumbled,
Smiling Lulu rocked and crumbled,
Weak with groans and laughter.

Luscious Lulu found her fellow,
No more would she bruise and bellow,
Softened to a warm marshmallow,
Happy ever after…

Dan Lake

The Moon Maid

The crescent of the moon drifts high,
Across a sable velvet sky,
Where I shall hold her silver hand,
Then travel to the moon's own land.

She'll scoop me up and on a sigh,
We'll sail through stars to Gemini
And stroll on Neptune's rippling sand,
Then travel to the moon's own land.

Pluto will wave and Mars will call,
For he's the solar know it all
I'll marvel as I understand,
Then travel to the moon's own land

I'll serenade you with delight
And kiss the beauty of the night,
Deep scented with each starry strand,
Then travel to the moon's own land.

And as I'm shimmering aloft,
With sequins glittering so soft,
I witness shooting stars disband,
Then travel to the moon's own land.

O'er silken skies where stars lie deep,
And o'er the land where you're asleep,
Your dreams I'll scatter as I planned,
Then travel to the moon's own land.

Lulu Gee

Patience Is a Virtue

How patient is the dog that sleeps before the fireside,
He misses boots and jangling leads now that his masters died,
He doesn't know he's passed away but knows his masters gone,
And stretches out contentedly and knows he won't be long.

His master wouldn't leave him, of this he is so sure,
He wags his tail and looks up every time he hears the door,
His days turn into weeks that turn to months as seasons pass,
But patience is a virtue and his loves not made of glass.

Many years have passed now and the dog has grown so old,
Then waiting by the fireside his heart grows still and cold.
He knew one day his man would come, he hears his master talk,
'Come on old lad it's been a while, we're going for a walk.'

Dan Lake

This Morning ....

This morning as I walked alone beneath clouds plumped with snow,
I heard a thousand voices, putting on a show,
Such loveliness surrounded me and for a while was mine,
As bullfinches played hide and seek, in a blue-jade pine.

A hawthorn made a canopy across the bridle path,
As robins in fine waistcoats, sought the magpie's wrath
And wagtails drank from icicles beneath the dry stone wall,
While bramblings looked for insects, succulent and small.

As cold winds kissed my forehead, to blow cobwebs away,
Snow fell soft and silent from clouds of silver grey,
To quickly cover drooping boughs and ferns in dappled light,
Set against the lonely brook, dazzling, cool and bright.

Then suddenly a fallow deer peered through the mottled grove,
Her coat the softest velvet, her eyes the deepest mauve,
I stood, still as a quiet mouse afraid to move until,
The freezing cold around me, gave a biting chill.

Below the paleness of the sky where soon the moon would shine,
The finches still were playing, in a blue-jade pine
And all the bright-eyed life astir came out to say goodbye
And I was blessed with joyfulness as sweet as apple-pie.

Lulu Gee

The Christmas Box

He slumped down after dinner in his chair,
his desert boots lazed on his crumpled bed.
He ran his fingers through his golden hair
as thoughts ran through his mind the Padre'd said.
Words of love and peace at Christmas time,
the mem'ry of our God Almighty's son,
the wise men and the star that seemed to shine,
now shone upon his ammo belt and gun.

The parcel sat, impelling and austere,
a present from a land so far away.
His head spun from the bourbon and strong beer
he'd drank while toasting absent friends today.
The wind blew sand against his frail abode
as he removed the lid from off the case;
a photograph escaped the heavy load
sent from another time, another place.

His wife and children smiled a glad hello;
he caught his breath and wiped a saddened tear.
The letter said they wanted him to know
how badly he was missed this time of year.
No longer able to control his pain
his tears fell unashamed upon a line,
the sentiments seem normal and mundane;
words simply written saying, 'they were fine.'

They told him how they missed their precious man,
they told him to take care and come home soon.
They told him they'd do anything they can;
they told him they'd prayed underneath his moon.
They told him there's a 'box' beneath the brandy,
under cards and socks sent by his mother;
neath the lovely Christmas cake and candy
crafted by his wife his darling lover.

The words said that this box contained her soul;
to give him strength when he was almost spent,

to be a portal, nay a wide threshold,
where he could walk to ease his raw torment.
The box contained her strength and will to live;
her fortitude that came from God above:
Put trust and faith within this grant I give
sent with resolve and strong undying love.

~

Never doubt the power in this tiny silver box
left beneath the cake and your mother's woollen socks.

Dan Lake

The Tired Bear

When honey bees tickle my nose
Just as I lay my head to dream,
Of salmon I hope to expose
Beneath the mountain in midstream.

My soft brown eyes open with rage
When honeybees tickle my nose,
For I'm a bear of tender age
And in the sun I like to doze.

I growl a snore with soft bellows
But cannot close my tired eyes,
When honeybees tickle my nose
And buzz demonic in the skies.

When finally I rest my head
I dream of honey, I suppose,
Instead of salmon over-fed
When honeybees tickle my nose.

Lulu Gee

Now and Then

The music was erotic as we floated in the stars,
We danced among a multitude in smoke from fat cigars.
Everything was distant as I looked into your eyes,
Those pools of clear blue water, holding love and sweet surprise.

Your perfume filled my head and mixed with champagne stole my soul,
Your smile now warmed my heart, a heart that once was dark as coal,
No one else existed as your ruby lips met mine,
They took me to another place, a portal lost in time.

Forty years flew back in time; we danced in Ronnie Scott's,
Brubeck playing on the stage and we're still in the spots,
I'm twenty five pounds lighter and you've just reached twenty one,
A far off day when we could sway, those memories were fun.

I've known you all my life my love but how our seeds were sown,
To dance with you this special night, so intimate, alone,
And though we took our separate paths through life's troubles and fear,
Our worlds collided once again to bring you ever near.

Life's a roller coaster, a huge circle from above,
But when you take off your soft gown I'm still consumed with love,
You come to me and I can see the woman you were then
And look to please and comfort you, my darling once again.

Never fear my darling dear I've always held your hand,
From now until forever, even in the Promised Land.

Dan Lake

A Call Girl's Diary

It's just another Sunday night
With tricks to turn before daylight,
I've rent to pay and kids to feed
And now my mum's an invalid.

It's just another Monday night
I'm sent to tease and then delight,
Some want it quick, some want it slow,
I do what's asked and then I go.

It's just another Tuesday night
I hope to God I'll be alright,
Last night I heard a girl got beat
And from a car thrown on the street.

It's just another Wednesday night
And business men need to ignite
Some thrills with pleasure to their lives,
You'd think they'd go home to their wives.

It's just another Thursday night
Just one to go, a socialite,
Who sits by day in Parliament,
By night debauched and decadent.

It's just another Friday night,
I'll kindle passions to excite
Men with whom I've no rapport,
Old men who like to call me whore!

It's just another working night,
When will I dance beneath moonlight?

Lulu Gee

The Garden Sparrow

I look upon my garden from my roost,
I see the other birds and they see me,
The blackbird with his orange beak
The coloured jay with piercing shriek
And tiny blue-tits playing in my tree.

The song-thrush sings a love song for his mate;
The chaffinch shows his colours pink and blue,
The kestrel watches from on high
It hovers in the bright blue sky,
With swallows as they make their grand debut.

But me, I'm just a humble little bird,
A sparrow, no fine voice or livery,
Starlings with their spangled breast
The robin with his crimson chest
And goldfinches display their fine beauty.

I sigh as I sit watching in the branches,
I envy all this talent on display,
But I shall sing my mating song
Until my sweetheart comes along
And steals my heart and brightens up my day.

Dan Lake

When He Returns

Her skin is golden as the shore,
With neither blemish nor a flaw,
On his return he'll gaze in awe,
When back from war, when back from war.

And in his arms she'll gently lay,
While in their dreams they'll castaway,
To love where palm trees softly sway
And dolphins play and dolphins play.

They'll be no talk of things aghast,
Or missions that have been broadcast,
Of comrades who have died too fast,
By bombs that blast, by bombs that blast.

At noon she got the telegram,
'Killed on patrol by Taliban,'
Now she's alone without her man,
Afghanistan, Afghanistan.

Lulu Gee

False Identity

He told me in much detail what had happened that dark night,
Many years ago in my sad life.
He told me I was far away, he'd drank Chateau Lafitte,
And eaten filet-mignon with my wife.
He told me how she looked enticing, radiant he said,
She'd laughed, when he'd recite an entendre,
When dancing he had held her close and let him kiss her lips
She'd melted in his arms seductively.

He told me many times when they'd settled in the car
How she'd reached across and kissed him hungrily,
She'd rubbed his thigh and whispered, 'let's go home my darling man,
I need to feel you deeply can't you see.'
He told me how she'd grasped his manhood, kissing in the hall,
How she'd ran up to her bathroom in delight,
How she'd stood there naked and said, 'do just what you will,'
How he'd tied her to the bed that awful night.
Like an animal he'd used her taking her to massive highs,
Her vulgar words urged him, 'take every part.'
Then lying satiated he had reached beneath the bed
And with a knife cut out her beating heart.

Now I sit here long convicted in my sad and lonely cell,
His cunning saw me blamed instead of he.
His lechery appeased, he's gone and left me in this hell,
Where doctors say of course, that he was me!

Dan Lake

The Little Folk (Muses)

I have so many little folk
Who live inside my head,
While some are sad, some like a joke,
A few fill me with dread.

One takes me over field and dell,
To maybe chase white deer,
Or over bridges by Brunel,
Of whom there's no compeer.

And then there's her that makes me wish,
For things I haven't got,
Like cocktail gowns in silks that swish
And cruises on a yacht.

One makes me dream of years gone by,
To times when I was sad,
To when I used to wonder why
I had the life I had.

Of course there's one who makes me see
The storms of snow that rage,
Who bids me dance in Neptune's sea,
With metaphors to wage.

These people in my head bounce round,
With words I can't ignore,
One told me of a fairy mound
With magic to explore.

One made me write of marching feet
And then a red beret,
He urged a soldier's brave heartbeat
Be penned without delay.

In haste I write of plants in bloom
And early morning dew,
And my dream house within a coomb,
Because they tell me to.

At times they get it awf'lly wrong,
which leads to bad critique,
They mess about the whole day long
with odes not quite Sapphic.

I'm forced to write of love's desire
And kisses sweet as wine,
Of one who sets my heart afire
And in whose eyes I shine.

They whisper to me night and day,
At all hours of the clock,
Demanding that I must obey,
Deterring writer's block!

Lulu Gee

Your Chatelaine

This short but well meaning quatrain,
Holds a message from me sent to you,
Not a message afresh or anew,
Just you'd tie me to your chatelaine.

Please tie me to your chatelaine,
So my love might hang right by your side,
I might be your love key or your guide,
So you'd use me again and again.

Please lock me, securely enchain,
Caress me with your lovely hips,
As I hang by your side your hand slips,
To your wonderful firm chatelaine.

So tie me to your chatelaine,
Empower me with your sweet heart
And the knowledge that we couldn't part,
As I hang by your side on your chain.

Dan Lake

A Day in the Life of...

I've only got one pair of hands
Though you think I've got three
As you sit watching Countdown
Relaxed on the settee
I walked the dogs this morning
In wind and heavy rain
Thank God it wasn't snowing
Or worse, a hurricane
I've sorted all the laundry
It's in the tumbler now
I s'pose I'll have to iron it
Albeit somehow
Sorry 'bout your lunch dear
You said it wasn't hot
But never mind, for dinner
I'll make a beef hotpot
I pruned the weeping willow
And weeded the front path
Oh! I forgot the mowing
ARE YOU HAVING A LAUGH?
I KNOW we have a blocked sink
I've got the plunger out
Now what's that you're saying?
You think you've got the gout
I KNOW we're out of milk dear
I'll just pop to the shop
Before I go I'll dust around
And give the floor a mop
Now the kitchen's spic and span
OH DAMN! I've broke a nail
AND NOW the dogs need walkies
In a forceful gale
I washed the supper dishes
While you watched the football
Now I'm so bloody tired
I need an overhaul
I've got a crate of beer in
So you're ok tonight

Of course you'll get drunk darling
(My God, you look a sight)
Now I'll just put the cat out
and retire to my bed
to dream of Robert Redford
but NOT the aforesaid!!

Lulu Gee

His Own Coquette

My new home was on Dartmoor,
Full of old world charm,
With low black beams and old day dreams
Exuding peace and calm.

The inglenook was large and worn,
The stairs were old and sweet,
Each time I raced or slowly paced
They sang of dancing feet.

My bedroom was encompassing,
A warm and tender girth,
The old oak bed I'm sure had led
To many a child's birth.

My first night was exciting,
My nightdress white and plain,
A bottle of wine, this book of mine,
Outside the wind and rain.

The old clock chimed eleven
And I wandered to my bed,
No counting sheep, I'm fast asleep
With romance in my head.

My dreams weren't disappointing
As his fingers touched my hair,
I had no fear while he was near,
This stranger from elsewhere.

Night after night he took me,
He filled my every need,
He used me and abused me
Rode me like his trusty steed.

I went to my bed earlier
And later I would rise,
His loins aroused we were espoused
He slipped between my thighs.

I couldn't leave my bedroom,
His love devoured me.
My constant need, his want to feed,
No matter how crudely.

They found me there one morning
I was lying soiled and grimed,
No thought of cost completely lost
With loving on my mind.

And now I sit in this small room,
Alone, no paramour,
He's firm cocooned in my bedroom
Back there in old Dartmoor.

They're trying to expunge him,
They think that I'll forget,
My Captain Kid, My own El Cid,
I'm his. His own coquette…

Dan Lake

When Tony Bennett Picks a Plum

When Tony Bennett picks a plum
From the tree of life,
As Frank Sinatra sings of sharks
Annoying Mack the knife,
Then asking me where are the clowns,
By the great Sondheim,
Then I won't write of poetry
That doesn't have a rhyme.

And when Dean Martin croons of things
It makes me want to cry,
Then with a whisky in his hand
He'll hum, I don't know why,
But when no mountain's high enough
For Gaye Marvin to climb,
Then I won't write of poetry
That doesn't have a rhyme.

When Sade says your love is king,
Just singing by your side,
Or when The Beatles ask for help
Wanting tickets to ride,
When Black Eyed Peas meet me halfway
And Pink Floyd echoes time,
Then I won't write of poetry
That doesn't have a rhyme.

If Streisand sings the way we were,
Or if you go away,
In the park on Sunday
When funny girl won't play,
Or when I hear of Bette Midler
Sing swinging from a vine,
Then I won't write of poetry
That doesn't have a rhyme.

When dying in your arms tonight
Means more than just a song,
As there's no more tomorrow
Because our life's been long,
When eulogies have all been said,
In spring or summertime,
Then I won't write of poetry
That doesn't have a rhyme.

Lulu Gee

Kissed the Wind

I watch you as I sit here, sing an armchair serenade,
Play music as you danced barefooted on the soft brocade,
Then stroll along the Norman ramparts on the Esplanade
And kissed the wind that sometimes passed us by.

You hold my arm your glowing charm is radiant and sweet,
We tried to dance and laughed perchance as I have two left feet,
Those passersby who smile and try to look and be discreet
Just kissed the wind that sometimes passed us by.

Though we are old we're not I'm told, too old to refrain yet,
We can smile and walk a mile and kiss with no regret,
Your laughter rings a blackbird sings a song we won't forget
We kissed the wind that sometimes passed us by.

Though time is short I care for nought as long as I have you,
Your love of fun brings out the sun when I am feeling blue,
The world will miss our tender kiss when it says, 'sad adieu'
Then kisses winds that sometimes passed us by.

Dan Lake

Tea for Two

Today is his birthday and this is his treat,
I promised to meet him out here on the street,
I'm dressed in my finest from head to my feet,
For afternoon Tea at The Ritz.

The maître d' greets us with courteous grace,
It's busy and bustling with organised pace,
As we take our seats amid cut glass and lace,
For afternoon Tea at The Ritz.

My beau's looking smart in his suit of cashmere,
And now he is smiling from ear to ear,
He blows me a kiss and says, 'thank you my dear,'
For afternoon Tea at The Ritz.

There is chicken and ham and egg dressed with cress,
Cucumber, cream cheese and salmon no less,
Served with elegance to befit a princess,
For afternoon Tea at The Ritz.

Our tea can be Jasmine, Lapsang or Chun Mee,
With fruits of the forest and fresh baked pastry,
We're treated like royalty, a gent and lady,
For afternoon Tea at The Ritz.

The Palm Court is splendid and one can see why
'No room for improvement,' I wink with a sigh!
As we take our leave and we say a goodbye,
To afternoon Tea at The Ritz.

Lulu Gee

The Moon & the Tree

I've watched you cross the heavens now
For such a long, long while,
Changing shape and texture
With that enigmatic smile,
While I've stood here tied to the ground,
By roots that help me grow,
Jealous, envious of you
For I know not where you go.

Some days I see you in the sky,
Then night times you're not there.
What places do you visit,
While I stand alone and glare.
I've waited counting years on years
To seize you in my arms
And now I'm just enraptured
With your tantalizing charms.

I won't let go my silver glow,
My seeds in you I'll shoot,
Then like my staid and clumsy frame.
You'll also grow a root.

Dan Lake

I'll Dance for You

I'll dance for you at breakfast
And I'll dance for you at tea
Whatever time you want me
Just make sure you have the fee

I am cheaper by the hour
But I'm sure we can concur
To come to some arrangement
As to dances you prefer

I'll dance for you at dinner
Or at midnight if you wish
Of course the price is dearer
If you want me outlandish

I used to be a showgirl
So I know what I must do
If you need some titillation
Then I need to wear frou frou

I've sequins gold and silver
And a feather for my hair
And fishnets to enhance me
for my first night premiere

Lulu Gee

The Wych Elm Tree

I walked the magic footpath of folklore from long ago,
Laughing to myself of tales of sinister romance,
The evenings warm the gentle tide allowed the trees to flow,
Where buttercups and elderflower performed a perverse dance.

I settled neath the Wych Elm tree and watched the world at play,
Related birds would show their gender with their singing theme,
I lapsed into a mellow trance and heard the Wych Elm say,
'To sleep my precious, just contrive to sleep perchance to dream.'

I dreamed my love was lying near with lips of burning fire,
She kissed me with the passion of a lover urging me,
She raised me with her skilful hands and burnt me with desire,
'Neath the branches of the fabled magic Wych Elm tree.

She raged her ardour over me, I'd given up my soul,
I tasted her, she tasted me, a mystical embrace,
We clasped each other desperately, I'd lost my self control,
Then looking at my lover saw a warted gruesome face.

A scream of desperation revealed terror in my voice
And heard the Wych Elm laughing as it held me in a fold
Of gossamer and grasses used by witchcraft as its choice,
Of manacles to hold my naked body to behold.

The Wych Elm moved and changed its shape into an aged crone,
She cackled at my manhood pointing with her branch like hand,
Although I lay in terror sobbing on the ground alone,
She raised her stinking skirts to reveal all she had planned.

Sickeningly she took me in her body made of bark
And screamed a terrifying sound of triumph chilling me.
I'd consummated this old witch, the truth was plain and stark
And watched in awe as purple flowers appeared on the tree.

The wind arose as morning came and blew my fettered chain,
Releasing me to run away afraid, as fast I could,
With images best not described inside my addled brain,
I vowed I'd never venture once again into that wood.

Dan Lake

Today

Today I've seen such lovely things
I never knew could be;
Sunlight golden upon a jar
Of honey from a bee.
Frosted snowflakes and geese in flight,
Over the Lammas land
And children laughing after school,
With books to understand.
A gift of flowers in a vase
With just one single rose,
Amongst tulips and daffodils
Under a pretty nose.
Bed linen crisp as falling snow
And pillows plumped for rest.
A sweater bought just yesterday,
For me to look my best.
A poem penned to make me smile,
Or maybe even sigh,
Then walking with the dogs today,
Smiles from a passer-by.
An avocado green and ripe
To make my taste buds flow,
The crossword in The Telegraph,
A button I must sew.

And all because my love kissed me.

Lulu Gee

Janis Joplin

You poured out your rage, as you stood on the stage,
Where you'd give everything you could use,
You screamed and you cried, as a part of you died;
Naked, as you sang out the blues.

'Ugly Duckling.' My rock n roll whore!
Smack'd out baby, you died on the floor.
'White Blues Momma,' you played out your part.
I had taken 'A Piece of Your Heart.'

Dan Lake

A Retourne to Autumn

How sombre are the mornings with skies so frosty cold,
as trees let fall their showers of reds and molten gold,
but over where my heart is the harvest is complete,
he's looking to the sunset at fields of gathered wheat.

As trees let fall their showers of reds and molten gold,
beneath the wind now stirring is something to behold,
and as the sheaves are gathered below the quiet hills,
My heart whispers a love song before the Autumn chills.

But over where my heart is the harvest is complete,
amid the fields of golden bronze all around his feet
and when the earth's in shadow beneath a lazy sky,
wood smoke lingers in the air as clouds unfold on high.

He's looking to the sunset at fields of gathered wheat,
where blackbirds have departed with appetites replete,
while gazing at his acres of which he'll never tire,
oh, if only I were there to quell my own desire.

Lulu Gee

The Birth of the Herald

Where fire eaters drowned she lifted it,
An unknown shape that once walked on this plane.
Kissing holes where'er the eyes had been,
She held the thing aloft to rise again.
As putrid drops of pus fell on her lips,
She cried intense for Lucifer to come,
Her work was never over for her here,
Ten thousand years she'd called the holy one.

Regaling lord and master to arise,
She laid the shapeless mass upon the throne,
Her bony naked body knelt to pray,
Her knees bled on the cold and heartless stone.
Tormented and demented she prayed on,
Hour after hour day on day,
Eternal in her quest to bring alive,
The memory of the thing she'd seen decay.

The fire and the brimstone burnt her throat,
A throat that garbled words of unknown source,
The pain within the shrine was so intense,
She shrieked the words beneath a demon force.
Between her legs a pool of blood appeared,
That stank of rancid bile and faecal waste,
And as she screamed in passion and distress,
She saw that her weak body had unlaced.

In the blood and gore of her debris,
A squirming shape that took no mortal form,
The head and feet were goat like though affixed
To the body a human she had borne.
She cried with glee at last her prayers were heard,
She knew the name of this thing she'd beget,
And held the tiny beast of pain aloft,
Then screamed the name, repeating Baphomet.

Baphomet the messenger had come,
To pave the way for Hades holy one.

Dan Lake

The Little Brown Tick

I'm sat atop this blade of grass,
And set to crawl as bold as brass
Onto a host, all fat and stocky,
Such as this puppy, Jabberwocky.
As he meanders in this glade,
I and the others will invade,
We don't sashay, skip, hop or fly
But suck up blood then multiply.

Now Jabberwock, will suit me well,
I will attach and create hell,
I'll crawl around until I reach
His nose, all squashy like a peach.
There's not a lot of people know
I'm an arachnid supremo,
Slowly I'll suckle his lifeblood
Without a please or thanks m'lud.

I'll feed here now for many a day
Before my batch of eggs I'll lay,
Young Jabber will feel under par,
Like old Chenille, the chihuahua,
Who also has a tick or two
And as eggs hatch they will accrue,
feasting on a feeding frenzy,
'Til revealed by vet McKenzie.

That old McKenzie hates us ticks,
It's perilous in his clinics,
But here I am on Jabber's nose,
And old McKenzie's in the throes
Of cruelly disengaging me,
As if I'm but an irritant flea,
Dislodged like vermin with aplomb,
Aha! There's more where I came from!!!

Lulu Gee

I Miss You So

I wake with you each morning and I miss you,
At breakfast we will chat but you're not there.
I ask about your latest, (for a preview,)
I smile and touch your hand, but its elsewhere.
Then over lunch we share a glass of merlot,
Discussing plants while eating cheese and ham,
The words seem true, but really I'm in limbo,
I wipe a tear, I don't know where I am.

You showed me where to plant the rose this morning,
Reminding me to feed and then to spray,
I'm talking to myself, (is this a warning,)
You say it looks like rain the sky is grey.
You smile and let me know that all is lovely,
A smile that always takes my breath away;
Your right about the rain the air is balmy,
We gather tools and put them all away.

The evening rain beats on the patient window,
Your music choice, it sounds like Simply Red,
We finish off the wine that leaves a warm glow,
You whisper that it's late and time for bed.
I lay and dream of all the things you bring me,
Such love and peace of mind for us to share,
I stretch my arm across the bed beside me,
Remembering those times when you were there.

Tomorrow we'll go fishing bright and early,
You tell me only if the weathers fair.

Dan Lake

Paradise Views

I'm on a desert Island; and have been here countless years,
I'm dreaming of horizons blue through soft abandoned tears.
'They' said things would improve if I moved to 'Paradise View,'
My house got far too big for me and this is quite bijou.
Now countless days' I'm sitting here just waiting all alone
But 'They' no longer visit me, nor do 'They' telephone.

I'm on a desert Island; and I've sat here countless years,
Just beneath a palm tree swaying through soft abandoned tears.
My hammock is an upright chair to ease my aching back,
The bath with handles on each side is my bright red kayak.
At times I glimpse a passing ship and cry, 'ahoy who's there,
Please will you come ashore today, come in, pull up a chair?'

I'm on a desert Island; I'm marooned here countless years,
I dream of an eternity, through soft, abandoned tears.
I have a nice Girl Friday who is from MacMillan's Trust,
She chuckles when I tell her of my thoughts of wanderlust.
But says it won't be too long now because that passing ship,
Is just offshore at anchor and awaits my final trip.

I'll leave this desert island where I've laid so many years,
I'm going now to Paradise where I'll shed no more tears.

Lulu Gee

The Clock Ticks On (Monotetra)

Before the dawn the blackbirds sing,
They sense the joy the day will bring;
Beyond first light they're on the wing,
Beyond the dawn, beyond the dawn.

Just as the sun creeps ever near,
Those bats and owls will disappear,
A notion of that golden sphere
Will see them gone, will see them gone.

Once more the photosphere will rise;
Alarm clocks ring to our surprise
And wake us from our deep demise,
To start the day, to start the day.

Kettles sing and showers rain;
We leave to earn our corn again;
The car won't start, we take the train,
The clock ticks on. The clock ticks on.

Then in a blink of times firm eye,
The sun will sink down in the sky
And yawning, there go you and I,
From whence we came from whence we came.

Dan Lake

Marching Feet

At the cenotaph we stand on this depressingly cold day,
Amid a sea of misery 'neath clouds of autumn grey.
The mood is darkly sombre with emotions riding high,
As the sound of distant marching feet causes me to sigh.

Like bloody corpses poppies strewn the cold grey cenotaph,
I can no longer read for tears the written epitaph,
The marching feet get closer as I hear the women weep,
For those who died in battle, now eternally asleep.

How many kisses never kissed or smiles no longer smiled,
Lay beneath conflicting lands so brutally defiled,
How many promises not kept or letters not received,
How many saddened spouses, forsakenly aggrieved.

The Royal Marines take the salute, leading the marching feet,
Old soldiers, some in wheelchairs march to, 'Beating Retreat,'
Caps and medals proudly worn and boots enhanced with shine,
With every single soldier marching in perfect time.

Now I am weeping openly, my heart feels like a vice,
To think these men laid down their lives for us and at what price,
Our children and our grandchildren can live a life that's free,
From tyrannical oppression they will not have to flee.

The only sounds I hear today are those of marching feet,
Of men and women crying at the melancholy beat,
For all those that are falling still that we may live in peace,
Oh! Please God when will it stop .... When will the fighting cease?

Lulu Gee

My Bin Just Needs Relief!

It sits there grimacing in pain, loaded to the hilt,
I've rammed and crushed the rubbish in for fear that some is spilt,
It pleads for mercy bursting, bloated, wheels that sit awry,
With all the insects in my yard all knowing where to fly.

I'd take it to the doctors but I just might upset him,
Towing half a ton of rubbish in a wheelie bin,
'Can you cure indigestion,' (it's a nasty shade of green,)
'One more teabags all it needs to rupture wheelies spleen.'

Just where can I take him, to relieve him of his pain,
I took him to the local dump (who sent me home again,)
They said they can't take rubbish, that's not what they're for,
The bins not the right colour and they'd break the EU law.

My bin just needs relief! Some Liver-salts might help,
I half expect it to cry out, some whine or maybe yelp.
But quietly it sits there in a sorry mortal haze,
But the poor thing has to suffer for another seven days.

Dan Lake

To Dream of You

As I arrange my tousled curls upon a silken rest,
  to dream of you so tranquil with your head upon my breast.
I lie beside you naked that your eyes alone may see,
  this woman who you say you love, the secret core of me.

I am no longer young my darling neither am I old,
  the fires of love still burn and they keep me from the cold.
While flushed I am with passion for reasons you bestow,
  as here we lie as lovers, flesh aflame in afterglow.

I dream of you at sunrise and when the evening's cold,
  when the leaves are lush and green or when they're turning gold.
My dreams are now but moments, just grains of granuled sand,
  as on the tide they ebb and flow I seek to kiss your hand.

I come to you my darling with naught but joyous love,
  as tenderly you cherish me 'neath velvet skies above.
To hear you say you love me and I am your Faberge
  brings tears of such sweet happiness and dreams of you this day.

Lulu Gee

The Toast

I am an Englishman by birth my colour matters not,
My father fought for what I have and ne're shall be forgot,
When proud men pass the cenotaph the brave beside the braves
With memories of battle's fought, and comrade's in their graves.

From India to Africa, Korea across to Spain,
In Swampland's of America in France and home again,
From Canada to Germany to Israel in the sands,
A British soldier lies at peace among these foreign lands.

They asked for naught and gave their all for us in our dear home,
So Briton you may come from and in Briton you may roam,
Freedom's what they died for, a freedom that won't yield,
These men lay in a corner of a 'Ne're Forgotten Field.'

These men come from far corners, of our proud GB,
Proud of ancient regiments, of Planes and ships at sea,
English, Irish, Welsh and Scots, homelands they will cheer,
For they are ancient kingdoms, and their kingdoms they hold dear.

St. David's Day it comes to pass proud welsh men raise their voice,
St. Andrew's is when Scots men drink the nectar of their choice,
The Irish bless St Patrick so I fear that I must say:
I'll drink a toast to English men, 'On this St George's Day.'

Dan Lake

An August Storm

The winds are strong and blowing cold,
in skies that brood and cry today,
for while the leaves turn coppery gold,
the august warmth is cast away.

I pray the winds will cease to blow
the fragile spider webs now spun,
through the fruit trees row on row,
where harvesting has now begun.

How silenced are the birds that sang,
by bugle blasts of stormy rage,
beside the cricket chants that rang,
as now the gale is centre stage.

For hours the rolling clouds sail by,
afar from yonder northern sea,
where ships beneath a rainstorm sky,
must steer their courses steadily.

Now as the wind and rain has passed,
the calm shall touch my thankful breast,
when once again there's peace at last,
for us to lay our heads to rest.

Lulu Gee

Bewitching Hours

That moment when thoughts turns to dream;
When sleep arrives but hasn't blessed,
Your conscious mind is changing theme
Those floating moments you've caressed;
He comes without your soft behest.

He whispers that his minds possessed
He calls your name, he must extol
You, watch him as he slow undressed
While pledging love and pledging soul,
His beauty leaves you no control.

His agile frame, his hair like coal,
His eyes that burn with deep desire.
You can't resist he'll reach his goal;
His lips will set your heart afire,
You'll kiss his temple, climb his spire.

You touch those stars you so admire;
He takes you up where you belong,
Ever upwards ever higher,
With no remorse, no right or wrong,
You drift to sleep and he is gone;

You dream of him those dark hours long
He comes and goes all through the night,
You sing to him your sensuous song;
He serves you with complete delight.
Those witching hours of sweet excite
Slow glides away, your loving swan…

Dan Lake

Men of a Certain Age

Why do men of a certain age
Lust for a page three scorcher
Or bimbo's with enormous boobs
(Who've gone through pain and torture)
These men who've seen the best of days
Want young girls to desire -
With teeth perfectly straight and white
And skin so taut in jeans so tight
With bums as hard as Bakelite
To set old flames afire

Why do men of a certain age
Lust for a page three beauty
Or Dollies tanned with bleach blonde hair
Who like to shake their booty
These men who've seen the best of days
Want to recapture youth -
By having a sex fuelled affair
With a thong covered derriere
Behind closed doors and portiere
They're crazy ...... that's the truth?

Lulu Gee

How to Dance (Sarabande Sonnet)

She sang 'You taught me how to dance,'
Delightful, seeking to beguile,
For I knew nothing of romance.

You took my hand I saw you smile,
That smile that reassured my heart,
That smile that said we'd never part
You said, 'come sir, we'll dance awhile.'

There in that dance of life I found
A course beyond my turbulence,
A harbour that's both safe and sound.

I'm glad 'You taught me how to dance'
And darling as I dance with you,
I'm gliding as if in a trance;
To that old world I say, adieu.

I have a life, I'm now aware,
For I have you; and love to share.

Dan Lake

Please Tell Me?

It's such a tiresome thing to do
To lie and watch the whole night through
When frightening nightmares over-run
But soothing comfort there is none
Instead I feel a lingering death
Why can't I hear another's breathe
Why can't I bathe my desperate soul
Or ease my aching limbs with oil
Morning and night they are the same
Where is life's vibrancy and flame
I hear songbirds but not their song
I must have done something so wrong

And when the morn brings tears for kin
Please tell me where life will begin

Lulu Gee

The Bluebells (sonnet)

In carpets of blues beneath the tall beech,
Anemone's play springing from sweet tears;
The emerald hues on high out of reach,
While time circles sway over thousands of years.

The clock ticks away as the sun slowly swings
The lazuline sky brings life to the scene.
A fervent bouquet from bells as they ring
Brings tears to the eye in this locale serene.

As far as I see the tall bluebells dance,
While butterflies drink in eternal largess,
No wonder birds sing as they seek to enhance,
While nature applies her last touch to her dress.

I revere this moment, this window in time
And will firm lock away in this memory of mine.

Dan Lake

First Light

Now the moon has disappeared and the stars have lost their shine
And I feel you at the breaking of the day,
As I put my arms around you and our bodies realign;
I can smell the muskiness of Faberge.

As the misty grey of morning brings a chill into the room,
I can sense a little shiver down my spine,
It is always like the first time when you were my shy bridegroom;
When you uttered words of love that were divine.

But now the sun has risen and her warmth is everywhere
And my breath is coming just a little fast,
You can write a magnum opus and each times a premiere,
As we never see shows with an undercast.

And now daylight has broken and the sun is streaming through,
As we linger for an extra moment more,
Before you go into the bathroom and call for more shampoo,
My love for you oozes from every pore.

Lulu Gee

My Doreen

I thought that I might take me down to London,
The local lads said that's the place to go,
Before I reach the ancient age of thirty,
I'd got some oats I'd rather like to sow

I travelled down by train, you won't believe,
I went on something called the underground,
And with the help of a nice lad called Georgie,
Arrived in Piccadilly safe and sound.

The strangest chap! He wore women's attire,
He said his togs were stolen from his line;
The poor lad has been treated rather badly,
So gave him fifty quid and duds of mine.

He disappeared soon after, what a darling,
He rushed to get himself some decent clothes,
But not before he kissed me rather strangely,
(It's how they say goodbye one must suppose.)

He'd given me a card of a sweet lady,
It says her name is Doreen that sounds nice,
I'm standing at her front door and I'm nervous,
I wish someone could give me some advice.

The door opens and there stands my young maiden,
With Marlene Deitrich looks and robust voice,
Her golden hair cascades down to her shoulders,
(The size of her large feet is not my choice.)

But I am smitten, I can't help but love her,
She's everything and more that I desire,
She swiped my credit card and sat beside me,
I knew she was the one to light my fire.

Her kisses were like heaven but her stubble,
Was something I'd get used to in a while,
But when I showed her what this man was made of,
Her large hands soft caressed me so servile.

A marriage made in heaven's what they call it,
We've everything we need, life's so sublime,
But I'm still wary touching her appendage,
Because it seems to be a lot like mine.

Dan Lake

We Need to Talk

We need to talk of oh, so many things,
of winters past but still a host of springs
when daffodils will in a crescent sprawl
and grasses eager start to grow so tall.

We need our hearts to hear a golden song,
as nightingales sing all the summer long,
on avenues that glisten in the mist,
then in a cloudless sky are sunshine-kissed.

We need to see afar beyond our eyes,
sweet roses scattered in translucent skies,
or sunlight pouring gold on fields of corn
for birds with beating wings in early dawn.

We need our love to guide us through the years
and yet be not afraid to shroud our tears,
as hand in hand we'll cast for dreams in sight,
beneath a distant moon in sequinned night.

We need to talk of oh, so many things,
of winters, summers, falls and joyous springs.

Lulu Gee

Our Sovereign's Gates

Our sovereign's gates swung wide, unbarred,
as we drove in the palace yard,
a poetess and dubious bard,
ebulliently.

The splendour in the regal hall,
the paintings on the textured wall,
located to enhance, enthral,
impressed me.

The gold leaf on the Georgian chairs,
and carpets on perpetual stairs,
where regal feet of regal heirs,
go blithely.

Beefeaters in garish clothes,
footmen ever on their toes
discreet and tactful, (I suppose,)
smile brightly.

Film stars on the sumptuous lawn
mix with old men, tired who yawn,
who landed on Juno at dawn,
so bravely

Young men, crippled smiling gay
who most enjoy this special day,
who lost their limbs so far away,
from Blighty.

Honours worn on chests with pride,
by men who'd watched as friends had died,
tortured souls who often cried,
some daily

Mothers, widows, anxious, shy,
stand proudly, but their smiles belie,
their painful loss and times they'd cry,
some nightly.

So who am I among this throng,
these heroes all, I don't belong,
as bandsmen play a cheerful song,
politely.

Dan Lake

Acorns

Fragile little fairy folk,
Toss the acorns in the air,
Just before a wintery cloak,
Covers autumn with despair.

Elfin poised with gentle grace,
Acorns wreathed upon her brow,
With a tireless, dancing pace
Harvesting the oaks right now.

Deer and jays turn up to dine
And with squirrels join the queue,
'Round the roots that so entwine,
Acorns fresh on the menu.

Little mice still linger on,
'Neath the boughs of oak they creep,
Then with fairies one by one,
With their acorns slumber deep.

Lulu Gee

The Sad Cortège

Young bloods spilt in far off places,
Shattered dreams in shattered faces,
Whose warm smile alone replaces
Those that can't complain.

The piper plays a lone refrain,
When souls are brought back home again,
Where mothers try to best explain
To children's bemused ears.

The cortège bedecked with the tears
Of flowers thrown from far frontiers
As has done now for many years,
In Wooton Bassett's street.

Old soldiers stand with aching feet
With shoppers in the road replete,
With widows weeping bittersweet,
Their loved ones draped in flags.

Then once again those fervent lags
Procession gone, search in their bags,
For handkerchiefs and calming fags,
Wish for this all to end…

Dan Lake

It's Two in the Morning

Now it's two in the morning and I'm still awake,
I'm sure I won't sleep till I see the daybreak,
I've tossed, I've turned and twisted all night
And I'm itching like mad 'cos a gnat's had a bite.

I'm hot, then cold and have fidgety legs,
So at three I get up to make soft scrambled eggs.
But the smell of the eggs and the hot buttered toast
Has awakened the dogs, sleeping by the bedpost.

To each dog I give biscuits to settle them down,
While dribbling hot coffee down my dressing gown!
I curse, 'bloody hell,' what am I doing here?
I'll go back to bed and simply persevere.

So I'm back in my bed and it's ten after five,
I've cooked and cleaned therefore in overdrive,
But still I can't sleep so I turn on the telly,
To hear bad news of an earthquake in Delhi!

I see Gordon Brown looking evermore shifty,
He's whinging by saying, 'we must be more thrifty'
He'll okay more payouts for banking bigwigs,
Then sanction expenses for MP's shindigs.

This news is depressing; so I'll bathe and dress,
It's too late to sleep and I'm under duress.
The dogs whine and howl as I tug my skirt zip
They want their 'walkies' but I want to kip!

I think about politics, (maybe I'll stand)
And speak for the working man of this great land,
There's oodles to do before the election,
I'll clean up the chaos of Brown's interjection!

Should I be elected I need beauty sleep,
My eyes are too weary to count endless sheep,
So if you don't mind, I'll wish you goodnight,
Please don't Email or phone for at least a fortnight!!!!!

Sshhhhhhh...

Lulu Gee

How Many Times

How many times she's brushed my lips,
With cheek and palm and fingertips
How many times we've loved and quenched our thirst.
How many times she's shed a tear,
While whispering love in my ear,
No matter, for it's always like the first.

She's touched my breast with hands that are electric,
She whispers words of love and strokes my hair,
Without her I'm a drum that has no drumstick,
Like air I breathe I know she's always there.
How many times will tenderness surpass,
Submitting then to time, like broken glass.

Dan Lake

Our Dream House

There is a house within our dreams
  Near a field of rye,
Tranquilly it waits for us,
  This house, we'd love to buy.
It slumbers in a copper wood
  Bright as a polished jewel,
Which needs to be reset in gold
  For rebirth and renewal.

This house that's nestling in a vale
  Is kissed by sloping hills,
Where cattle hug surrounding fields
  Amongst wild daffodils.
Such joyfulness should fill this house
  With laughter, love and care,
Someone to bring it back to life
  With happiness to spare.

This house that blinds us with its light
  Is statuesque and grand,
It has been empty these past years
  Just waiting for my hand,
And by a weeping willow tree
  There is a wooden seat,
That's wide enough to cuddle you
  And rest our weary feet.

This house, we'll fill with memories,
  And fabrics in rich hues,
Silky brocades and velveteen's
  And ornate curlicues.
We'll cast a spell upon this house
  To let the sun seep through,
Upon the floors of polished oak
  And doors of palest yew.

This house should brim over with flowers
  On tops ashine with wax,
Wild marguerites, picked on our walk
  Arranged with golden flax,
And when the moon is riding high
  These pleasures we will own,
To watch the sunset sink below
  No ruin - but our home.

Lulu Gee

Evil Dreams

Where paths may cross and re-cross yet again,
Where angels fly with dragon's wings and curse,
When darkness falls around the devil's train,
And monk's with gleaming eyes become your nurse.
She lay spread eagled, tied with chained regimes,
A crown of thorns bedecked her bloodied face,
That night when you confronted evil dreams,
You stroked her body with your burning mace.

Her lips were twisted painted with desire,
She screamed in pain and begged you to engorge,
She has no will save you to fan her fire,
Her demon eyes, they beg you to re-forge.
The tabernacle dripped with painless blood,
That runs from open tears in soft white skin,
All mixed with shitty rags and putrid mud,
Then entered to the underworld within.

You draw the mace across those painted lips,
Her bleeding tongue licked greedy on its path,
Across the crown of hell she slowly sips
Then baring canine teeth she starts to laugh.
She screeches, 'fool you think you control me,
I have what you desire there below.
Now use your burning mace and set me free,
Compared to me you're as the driven snow.'

I'll never try to please that bitch again,
I'm destitute and ruptured, wracked with pain.

Dan Lake

Lament for a Red Beret (Afghanistan)

Go forward brave Paras, step into the breach,
Our bravest young men going out of our reach,
Our tears and embraces must now see you through,
For God knows how long, oh if we only knew.

Go follow your orders, you've sung lullabies
To your young babies with tears in your eyes,
Your spirits will help you to campaign with pride,
Returning heroic and more dignified.

Go with our love lads, we wish you all well,
As you take command in Afghanistan's hell,
You'll go on patrols into hostile terrain,
Where the Taliban threat is so bloody insane!

Go into the wilderness of that far land,
When you come home lads you'll have a riband,
Another new medal, a further war fought,
Another stop press on a newsreel report.

Go valiant Paras into the hot sun,
Where food is deprived and you sleep with your gun,
Trek over the hill lads and that far ravine,
But watch where you tread for landmines are unseen.

Go pursue terrorists and the ringleader,
As you sought Hitler ..... go seek Al Queda,
Advance into battle with God by your side,
And Angels above you to guard and to guide.

Go onward brave Paras to seek out the scourge,
Of raging insurgents, we'll sing you a dirge.
Your Red Berets wear with the highest esteem,
Maintaining your goals as you scream and blaspheme.

Go seek out your chaplain, kneel with him in prayer,
Making some sense of this bloody warfare!
‘Beat the Retreat’ Paras, enough has been said,
Another Red Beret’s among our war dead.
Amen

Lulu Gee

Rugger Buggers

The manager has failed again,
It looks as though he's lost his reign,
He's sacked and really can't complain,
A shame but that's rugby.

The teams all called to Twickenham,
The home of England's failed Grand Slam
To meet the new mentor, 'main man?'
He's called, why? Lulu Gee!!!!

This he's a she, you hear them cry,
As up the tunnel players fly
And pundits hold their heads and sigh,
It's plain for all to see.

She sits them down and wipes her skirt,
(she can't resist the chance to flirt)
While players look, try to avert
Their eyes from her beauty.

She speaks with prestige and aplomb
And points out where their games gone wrong,
'It's rugby not a damn sit com!!!
On that you must agree.'

'Rugger buggers, are rarely clean,
I'm talking to the whole fifteen,
Your mums have told me this damn team
Should wash,' she said blithely.

'We'll meet out here within the hour,
(for I shall join you in the shower)
And show you how I shall empower
You,' she thought rudely.

Now to a man they did respond,
For she had waved her magic wand,
She somehow got the lads to bond,
In perpetuity.

Now once again this mighty land,
It's team run's out, it's fire's fanned,
By Lulu Gee so neatly planned,
Those lads are putty in her hand,
(They're feeling good) and looking grand,
Winning for their country.

She's carried high down to the bath,
she knows the way, that worn footpath,
she'll join her boys and have a laugh
and hold their warm trophy's!!

Dan Lake

What Shall I Do?

What shall I do my darling, when
The winter comes by us again
When all the garden is asleep
And creatures are in burrows deep
If violets no longer bloom
Then everything is doom and gloom
When one by one the leaves fall down
As autumn's taken off her crown
When rivers iced, no longer stream
So can't reflect a sweet moonbeam
When there's no sign of sun or thaw
And I still miss you ... more and more

When golden days are black as night
So there's no warmth to cause delight
Or when the birds with feathers fluffed
No longer sing with hearts so chuffed
And Santa's polishing his sleigh
And I'm lonely on Christmas Day
When thunder strikes with veils of rain
To lash against my windowpane
And waves curl round the windswept bay
And still you're very far away
When snow is two foot at my door
And I still miss you ... more and more

What shall I do my darling?

Lulu Gee

Your smiles

God made me a carpenter, he blessed my hands with wood
Making tables, bureaus, chairs and beds, most anything I could,
Bow fronted chests of draws in yew and rosewood's fine veneers,
Those bedroom suites and writing slopes all made along the years.

Secret drawers in cabinets, spring loaded with a catch,
To press a hidden button or to pull a harmless latch.
All these things I've crafted in the woods of finest kind
But one thing that escapes me is in progress in my mind.

I'll make a box from gossamer, veneers of cochineal,
Escutcheon made from teardrops, the inlays oh so tranquil,
When turned the key of moonbeams would reveal a billion smiles,
Collected when you passed my way through frankincense turnstiles.

Dan Lake

Beneath My Willow Tree

As I slowly close my book beneath my willow tree I look
at all the sumptuous coloured springtime gifts,
of daffodils in golden gowns, not for them poor hand me downs
and primroses amassed in fertile drifts.

There are magpies and they stand like a military band,
while whistling they strum a happy tune,
and robin redbreasts full of praise for the end of stormy days
as spring is here and not an hour too soon.

The air is warmer by the day as I watch a chaffinch play,
beneath the weeping willow where I sit
and sparrows lovelier by far than they really think they are,
are curious and look for a titbit.

Over where my hammock swings my cat is doing silly things,
he aims to catch a kingfisher in flight.
It is lovely here to lie and watch the bees and dragonfly
and view these wondrous things within my sight.

I hear bells ring out for church and I see catkins on the birch
while blossoms burst their buds for butterflies.
When my friends drop by for tea we sit beneath my willow tree
and mallard chicks appear with hungry cries.

Now as I open up my book beneath my willow tree I look
to read a page on springtime poetry,
but digress with John McCrae and Flanders Fields where poppies lay
and nature bows her head respectfully.

Lulu Gee

Those First Moments

That first blushing of caress, that first meeting of the eye,
Those first words that you express, those few seconds you comply,
When you don't want to seem forward but neither dull nor shy,
Those first moments, those first dawning seeds of love.

That first accidental touch of those waiting fingertips,
Those words that mean so much from their warm and tender lips,
A collision on life's ocean and the sinking of two ships;
Those first moments, those first spawning seeds of love.

That first moment you're alone, those first flames of sweet desire,
Those first kisses you condone; those next kisses you desire,
For passions are aroused, it's so hard to quell the fire,
Those first moments, those first glowing seeds of love.

That first moment you're undressed when your thigh lays warm on thigh,
Those first moments you caress, hard on soft meets with a sigh,
When you lay entwined in afterglow, when love you can't deny,
Those first moments, those first growing seeds of love.

Dan Lake

Alexandria Parkes

His name is Alexandria Parkes,
Some think he works at Marks and Sparks,
By day a house husband of three
Out with his dog and his Frisbee,
No-one gives a second look
As in the park he reads his book,
He likes murder or mystery,
But just sometimes it's history.

At four his kids come home from school,
With tales of whose had the ferule
And was it John, or was it Jane
Who went home lunchtime with a pain.
He helps with homework best he can
While tossing omelettes in the pan,
And then its kisses at bedtime,
With stories and a nursery rhyme.

It's then he takes his reticule
And in blue jeans and red cagoule,
Will start his little fiat car
And drive up west, where he's a star.
His transformation will astound
And leave you feeling quite spellbound,
Because with sequins white as pearl
He's headlining as a showgirl.

With twirls and whirls in silver shoes
And wigs of curls in many hues,
He'll dance until the audience
Have encored for his radiance.
Then as the spotlight dims its light
He heads for home in dead of night.

His name is Alexandria Parkes,
Some think he works at Marks and Sparks.

Lulu Gee & Dan Lake

Her Fallen Angel

He is her fallen Angel;
She's his one salvation,
The sun and moon, midnight high noon
At one with inspiration.

Apart their lives were pointless
They were empty, weak, futile,
Together royal, regal, loyal,
Strong in thought, virile.

They're the war and peace of heaven,
They're the chalk and cheese of hell,
They compliment, their souls cement,
United to excel.

As lovers they are moulded
In their equilibrium,
Seeking appease, a need to please,
Perfection in the sum.

Two souls that need each other,
Born from the stars above,
Have found their place, as one they face,
A future built on love…

Dan Lake

My Golden Sailing Ships

I never like to go to bed,
Not since I grew so old,
So now I sleep in attic space
Where dreams can be tenfold,
For all the sky is there to see,
Especially the moon
Tossing about in velvet skies,
While laughing at Neptune.

A golden ship sails past my head
And then I see a fleet,
With golden oars sweeping the waves
In time to a drumbeat.
Their topsails pale as saffron spice
Cutting the waters steep,
Making the bows move steadily
But still not coaxing sleep.

I hear soft voices from the ships,
Speaking in foreign tongue
And smell the spices from far lands
And feel cloths of shantung.
Atop the masts silk pennons sweep
Across a liquid sky,
As topsails crack in wailing winds
Above me where I lie.

The wind rattles my windowpanes
But my heart isn't here,
It's on a golden sailing ship
With one that I hold dear,
Sailing away to happiness
Where lesser perils lie,
Where rainbow's end is at my door
And it's a sin to cry.

Soft shadows play upon my walls
Now not a sound I hear,
As silently my sailing ships
Pilot the exosphere,
As warm and drowsy from my bed
I watch the fleet sail west,
To navigate horizons new,
Till sleep takes me to rest.

Lulu Gee

Another Day

We sat there through that dirty night,
Smoking fags through lips drawn tight
Cuddling tin mugs charged with tea.
Another bite, another flea.

The thunder from our guns went on
As they had done so all day long,
The constant shaking of the ground
With every discharge, every round.

A nervous laugh, a joke was told
All heard before a thousand fold.
This rain it's turned the earth to glue,
Sinking, stinking, sucking you.

We shivered, chilled, or was it fright?
We're going over at daylight.
What will happen? We can't say,
Another push. 'Another Day.'

Dan Lake

Pearls of Rain

Supple and slim in ev'ry limb,
Ablaze with warm desire,
Fine lace perfumes, wholly consumes
A flame that won't expire.

Beneath the stars we think are ours,
Ashine like molten gold,
A naked touch can prove too much,
As loving hours unfold.

Soft tears again like pearls of rain,
Glimpsed through a mist at sea,
I see a smile and for a while
There's only you and me.

With swaying hips and kissing lips
As sweet as sugar spun,
And whisp'ring sighs into veiled eyes
Say, 'you're the only one.'

Lulu Gee

Retribution

'Shame on you,' the stern judge cried
'I'm outraged by your lies,
That's one thing that I can't abide
I'll send you to assize,
There my man you'll mend your ways
Your punishment severe,
You'll spend at least five hundred days
And hopefully two years.'

My cell was cold, the cell was small,
With cellmates mean and cruel.
They taught me to come when I'm called
They used me as a tool.
My nights were long and full of pain
My days I'd just endure,
I'd learned that I dare not complain,
I looked for a saviour.

He wasn't harsh nor was he grim
Nor was he fine and rich,
In fact I was his girl to him,
(His special little bitch.)
He'd dress me in girl's underwear,
He'd tie me with his chain,
He'd violate me on his chair,
He'd get inside my brain.

Now I stand in Leicester square
A rent boy dressed in drag,
When once I was a normal man
I'm just somebody's fag…

One day he stood before me and
I let him buy my ware,
That judge that sentenced me so grand,
Who cast me to despair.
And as he took me from behind
There in the gent's small stalls,
I reached between my legs to grip,
Then cut off both his balls!!

Dan Lake

Whisper True

Please my darling catch my breath,
Hear it beat until my death
And feel my love surround you
Whisper true.

Tears are falling softly now,
As you kiss my worried brow
And feel my love surround you
Whisper true.

See the moon nod with a sigh,
Just above in half the sky
And feel my love surround you
Whisper true.

Lay your head to gently rest,
With a kiss upon my breast
And feel my love surround you
Whisper true.

Say not that we love too much,
Take my heart with joy and touch
And feel my love surround you
Whisper true.

When the reaper wakes from sleep,
Calling me, my soul to keep,
Then feel my love surround you
Whisper true.

Lulu Gee

My Trijan Refrain (I suppose)

Is wonderment an earthly boon
When children look in awe,
Do angels round the lovers swoon
Depending what they saw.
Do mountains rush down to the sea,
Do deserts flourish round the tree,
I need to know
I need to know
To save my sanity!

Do stars appear in sunny skies,
Do crocodiles take fright,
Are raindrops when an angel cries,
Has atlas so much might.
Questions, questions in my head,
I think too much it's often said,
Is Darwin right
Is Darwin right
Is Genesis misread.

Can love define a tennis score
Or have we got it wrong,
When Stevie sings 'Cherie amour'
Is it a tennis song.
'My love is like a red, red rose,'
(Is love so thorny heaven knows)
Should I go back
and re-compose,

Is this a Trijan (I suppose).

Dan Lake

My Childhood

When I was young there were no trees
I don't remember soft warm knees
Or any kindness in a voice
Or any song that would rejoice

My father would bellow and cry
But as a child I knew not why
His temper always at the boil
But he was deaf, so in turmoil

My mother also cried a lot
But somehow didn't give a jot
I don't remember arms that cared
Only bad moods with nostrils flared

My playmate was a big 'black dog'
Not for me, dolls or leapfrog
A hand that slapped and caused me pain
My parents arguing again

No-one but no-one seemed to care
As I cowered behind a chair
The 'black dog' sitting on my knee
The only one to care for me

In my deaf, silent world I cried
But nobody ever replied

Lulu Gee

The Mountain's Refrain

How long have you sat peering down
Without a smile without a frown,
High above yon Keswick town
To keep you occupied.
So regal, charming's what you seem,
While hiding sheep and mountain stream,
Tarn's and waterfalls that gleam,
Deep in your mountain side.

Surrounded by your mighty friends,
Your profile suits your soft wild bends,
Your high appearance often sends
Those feet to irritate.
Appearing easy to the rambler
Hiker and the ancient ambler,
Setting off to puff and clamber
O'er your vast estate.

Oh mighty Skiddaw let them see
How your mood changes on the scree,
How once you slow persuaded me,
To say my sad adieu.
I lay here in your mighty fell
I saw your heaven, found your hell:
Alone I cried my sad farewell,
Then slowly morphed to you.

Just be wary where you tread
We lie up here, the restless dead
And late at night it's oft times said
As winds blow frozen rain.

You'll hear our sad and lost refrain…

Dan Lake

The 11th Hour

It's at the cenotaph we stand,
With poppy wreaths to lay,
Where quiet skies have threats of rain,
On this Armistice Day.

Since 1920 we have prayed
For those sent off to wars,
To fight for freedom and our land,
Then die on foreign shores.

Some lie upon a windswept hill
But many in a grave,
Still side by side in comradeship,
All heroes and all brave.

Warm tears they'll never see from kin,
Nor taste love from a kiss,
Nor hear a baby's cry begin,
Nor walk softly in mist.

I give my prayers to countless names,
Marching in unity,
Held in the wind's own cool embrace,
For all eternity.

In silence and all shining plain,
Beneath the flags that fly,
Where all around are faces that
Must surely feel as I!

It's at the cenotaph we stand,
With poppy wreaths to lay,
Where quiet skies have threats of rain,
On this Armistice Day.

Lulu Gee

Frank Gifford (A soldier of WW1)

Your name is Francis Gifford and I see
your regiment the Buffs, firmly inscribed:
'A Man of Kent,' a lad who fought for me,
no mention though of how or where you died.

Sitting here beside your warm headstone,
I see you're just a boy on judgement day.
I wonder did you leave a girl at home
and promise you'd 'take care' while you're away.

It matters not how many years you've lain,
among your countless comrades now at peace,
but endless wars have come and gone again,
the reasons too complex to see them cease.

I wonder Frank, if you'd have done the same,
if then you had the providence to see,
the shape the world would take, would you feel shame?
I'm glad you never saw what came to be.

'The war to end all wars,' of course was lies!
Let's look for common sense and compromise…

Dan Lake

A Light Read

Late afternoon with Mills and Boon,
She cries a thousand tears,
For heroines in crinolines
In love with buccaneers.

Before twilight, a handsome knight
Will step right off the page,
While she sips tea, enthralled you see
With stories to assuage.

With hearts afire and grand desire
And scandals in the sun,
Each page she'll turn with great concern
For lovers on the run.

With tear filled eyes it signifies,
The final chapters read,
Late afternoon with Mills and Boon,
Who said romance was dead!!

Lulu Gee

Eventual Love

The cold of the juncture brought shiver and chill
And the raw breeze of winter kept love from me still,
It was late in the day, I was missing the thrill;
In my Autumn of misused refrain.

The water reflected my silent resign
To a life without love, in this sad heart of mine,
I'd no sense or notion, of warmth or sunshine;
In my Autumn that I might obtain.

I mused as I sat there and wished for a time,
The love that I'd missed in my long remote prime,
Would come to me finally and then be mine;
In my Autumn and be my cocaine.

The warmth from the sun as it shone in the mere
Reflected my spirit and raised my good cheer,
The wind drops its rancour then sunrays appear;
In my Autumn I want to contain.

They rose from the pool wrapping arms around me,
The kiss of the sunshine brought sparkle, beauty
And the love in its warmth that was given freely;
In my Autumn that seemed so mundane.

Dan Lake

I Love To See the Narrow Boats

I love to see the narrow boats,
Along the river Wey
And all the wildlife that I see
When walking every day,
I take the dogs to sit awhile
Just by the old lock gate
And watch the crayfish being caught,
By boys with smelly bait.

I love to see the water vole,
The otters and the mink,
The swans with young so downy white
And adders that just slink,
The cheeky little moorhen chicks,
The mallard and the coot,
But most of all the kingfisher
Clad in his turquoise suit.

I love to meet the other folk,
All busy having fun,
The fishermen with patience sit
Until the day is done
And dog walkers I've known for years,
With dogs I know by name,
Dogs of every size and breed
Enjoying the same game.

I love to see the boats that moor
And tether for the night,
Then smell their dinner being cooked
With laughter at twilight,
When badgers start to snuffle round,
While owls are drifting by
And sometimes if it's very quiet
You'll hear a moonbeam sigh.

Lulu Gee

Magical Memories (A Rondeau)

Ah, may we dance? You smiled, aglow,
A woman now, we danced, although
Within those fragile moments long,
That disappeared within that song,
To times that seemed so far ago.

The music from the radio
Would see me ask while bowing low,
To my princess in her sarong,
'Ah, may we dance?'

Then stepping on my brogues we'd flow,
Around the room, my shoes below
Your tiny feet could do no wrong,
Daughter and dad, the weak and strong,
The question asked from your hero,
'Ah, may we dance?'

Dan Lake

My Autumn

Almost a half a year's been spent
  I really can't say where it went,
But now the nights are damp with chills
  And pretty flowers have lost their frills.

Let blushing petals soft as silk
  And creamy roses pale as milk,
Shake off their gowns of summer bloom
  With ling'ring scents of sweet perfume.

While shadows soft play in the trees
  To murmur sighs upon each breeze,
As leaves of gold unfold from limbs
  Beneath a sky that shades and dims.

Fruit ripe and kissed in warm lit sun
  Whispers that harvest has begun,
And so as earth puts forth her yield,
  Young, handsome men garner each field,

And now more distant is the sight
  Of moonbeams in the cool of night,
For in the summer they'd drift high
  To glimmer from a star-filled sky.

So now I'll rest my eyes and wait
  For winter .... to unlock her gate.

Lulu Gee

That Moment

My heartbeat lessens to a pace,
My breath begins to slow,
I see contentment in your face,
Your skin is all aglow,
I wipe a tear from your sweet eye,
You stroke my tangled hair,
You murmur a contented sigh,
Our perspiration shared,

That moment of complete reward
That passion so declared.

Dan Lake

Without You

I sleep with you and wake with you
And yet you are not there,
My head is filled with thoughts of you,
There's nothing to compare.
I see your eyes beseeching me
And yet you're not in sight,
But you're the one I want to see,
Each hour throughout the night.

I wander through my day's routine
And try to do my best,
I sing and dance to a beguine
And hold you to my breast.
Sometimes I'll shed a little tear
And think of other things,
But like a childhood thought my dear,
The memory just clings.

Your love is bathing me in sun,
With shelter from the storm,
At last I have somewhere to run
And you to keep me warm.
My darling, please stay close to me,
As dawn is to the dew,
As nectar to the honey bee,
As flowers are to Kew.

I sleep with you and wake with you
And sometimes you are there,

Lulu Gee

If You Were Me

If you were me and I were you
What changes would you have to do
Curb my ranting, ease my prose,
Rest assured, wear smarter clothes,
If you were me would you be pleased,
Would my problems make yours more eased.

If I were you and you were me
What changes would there have to be,
Would you change my attitude,
Be more at ease or be less rude,
Or would you curb my lion's heart
And put the horse before the cart.

If I could view me from aside
Would I comply as you've implied,
Would I say, 'now come on Dan
Pull up your socks, shape up man,'
Or would I say with sympathy,
'Oh you be you and I'll be me.'

Dan Lake

The Unicorn

Here in the forest in dawn's early rain
I sigh, for I know what I'll see,
Hoping by magic to catch sight again,
The unicorn, haughty and free.
Her mane ruffles on the cold silent breeze,
In skies that are broody and deep,
With herons calling to whispering trees,
Awakening meadows from sleep.

She dwells in a land where dragons reside,
Where witches can cast you a spell
And goblins will curse and even provide
For wizards, some toads and cadelle.
Mention the unicorn, tales will unfold
Of spirits that come back to life,
To roam evermore with blood that is cold,
Thus causing encounters with strife.

Gold is her horn that glistens with sheen
And she's whiter than rippling sand,
All beauty is here that you've never seen,
For this is a magical land.
With nostrils aflare she looks to the sky
Whilst drinking the dew from the mist,
Then on turning around she looks in my eye
And like magic, I'm instantly kissed.

I stand here and watch without any fear,
As night with the day rendezvous,
For I never thought I'd ever get near
This legend that many pursue.
Her tail is now swishing with a new scent
And her ears are pricked for a chirr,
As I must depart with tears of content,
To treasure my memories of her.

Lulu Gee

Our Promised Land

Bent and weary stick in hand he walks the walk of men,
His tricorn hat sits jauntily on high,
Marching slowly out of step with comrades gnarled and aged,
His thoughts are full of young men, bye and bye.
His heavy coat of scarlet twill a coat he proudly wears,
Is decked with medals showing what he'd done,
No standing on a corner preaching freedom for this man,
He'd earned our freedom fighting with a gun.

A ghostly army marches past him quick of step, young boys,
Hardly shaving all a mother's son.
All left on the battle-field. Had all these died in vain?
Taken when their lives had just begun.
Our former soldier glanced emotive through a tearful eye,
Nods to faces known so long ago,
Young boys who'd left ploughs or lathes to learn the art of war,
Laying down their lives to fight the foe.

His shining boots reflect his chums, old soldiers never die,
It's said that they just simply fade away,
A country fit for heroes he was told he'd come home to,
A wry smile crossed his lips as bandsmen play.
Where were these freedoms? Won with blood, won with tears and pain,
Won by men on sea, in sky, and sand.
In steaming jungles far away, and muddy Belgian fields,
They died for this today; 'Our Promised Land.'

Dan Lake

Little Beaver

'Cross the plains of Oklahoma
You will hear a folklore tale,
Of a brave called Little Beaver,
For his magic they'll regale.
You will hear his name in lodges,
On the prairies, hot and dry,
In the wigwams of the chieftains
Telling trappers passing by.

While the elders of the nation
Who no longer ride to wars,
Will narrate of Little Beaver
To papooses of young squaws.
You will hear he's a brave hunter
With a spirit in his veins,
From across loud rushing rivers,
To the dry sequestered plains.

Far beyond the plains the forests,
With jade pine trees growing tall,
They will talk about his exploits,
From the spring through to the fall.
They will speak of warring parties
And the visions he foresaw,
Of forthcoming wars of nations,
'Neath the flight of the condor.

He saw dangers in a crystal,
That he wore next to his heart
And with hissing from winged serpents,
Such dangers he could impart.
For two sunsets Little Beaver
Gazed into his crystal heart
To foresee a trail of tears,
Where the mountain ranges start.

So he called the tribes to council
And with wisdom spoke in peace,
Telling of the hissing serpents
With their wings of deep cerise,
From the Mississippi river,
They would trek twelve thousand miles,
Little Beaver saw it clearly
When he saw the corpse stockpiles.

And some rode on mustang ponies
And some walked a darkened haze
Far beneath the eyes of eagles,
Where the bison freely graze
And the spirits looked upon them
As they smoked their pipes of peace,
As they smoked the pipes together,
Free of any war-paint grease.

And they marched with lack of water,
Overland and to the west
And they died in tens of thousands,
With their loved ones to their breast
And they said, farewell to rivers,
Where the hunting had begun
In the land of their forefathers,
Far beneath the rising sun

'Cross the plains of Oklahoma,
You will see the Cherokees
And you'll hear of Little Beaver
With his tragic prophesies.
You will also hear from Pawnee,
Kickapoos and Chickasaws,
Starved and beaten from their homelands
Exiled from their southern shores.

Lulu Gee

Dance

Call me and I'll swim across the ocean,
Ask and I would drink a poisoned potion,
Just smile and I will ever take a chance
To ask you if you'd love to have this dance.

Send me and I'll climb the highest mountain,
Whisper and I'll bring you Rome's sweet fountain,
I'd act the fool before the world and prance,
Just to take your hand that we might dance.

I'll lie prostrate before the congregation
And spit upon the flag of my great nation,
I'd walk across the fires of romance,
To take your hand and hear you say, 'let's dance.'

I'll try to dance as lightly as a feather,
I'd look into your eyes as we're together,
Arousing me with just the faintest glance
And mould our hearts forever as we dance,

Just one long dance…

Dan Lake

I wish I were a poetess

I wish I were a poetess,
To write of lazy summer days,
With picnics on a yellow beach
While watching quiet, lapping waves
And maidens who freckled by sun
Are sweet as pie and cherry- lipped,
Who stroll with lovers hand in hand
Beneath moonbeams silvery tipped.

And when the autumn shadows come
To blow away the leaves so green,
I'll write of clouds soft in the skies
O'er veils of rain on Halloween.
Or waking to a dew-lapped morn
Where gardens wish to sleep not stir,
Except for spiders spinning webs,
Except for mice with velvet fur.

My muse in winter's frost may sleep,
As will the hedgehogs under mould
Curl up and dream of seeds to eat,
'Neath warmer skies sprinkled with gold,
But I am greedy for a kiss
From stars that shimmer in the night,
Upon a land that's cold with snow,
Upon a land that's crisp and white.

In spring I'll see the fairies wake
To skim the air on dragonflies,
Bejewelled in greens and mystic blues
To halt my pen with blissful sighs.
I'll write of primroses in bloom,
Begowned in every shade of dress,
Then close my eyes perchance to dream ...
I wish I were a poetess.

Lulu Gee

Another Amputee

God bless you Harry Patch and Henry A, your time has come,
You war horses, you veterans, of Jutland and the Somme.
Your names are carved in history books; you've represented all
Those countless, ghostly faces who marched with you in Whitehall.

I see your cortege passing, many faces wiping tears
And understand your efforts that you've made over the years.
To tell all those who'd listen of the horrors of your war,
Of what your generation did and what you brave men saw.

I've seen the sheer frustration in your faces as you've said,
'There's no glory on the battlefield there's only wasted dead.'
Young sons of crying mothers, young husbands of young brides,
Young hopes and aspirations washed away on countless tides.

Those wasted and lost coevals, what did they all die for?
Not so their eyes might once more see this country go to war
And send their sons to fight again in fatal noxious games,
To die once more in Picardy and lands with foreign names.

The sirens wail again, another plague had gripped the world,
A bloody festering boil had burst, hatred had unfurled.
Would this go on forever, this pestilence of men,
Was this the legacy of man to die and die again.

Another war had ended, another call to arms,
Another politician calling young men from their farms.
Another faceless bureaucrat who controls what he spends
And as we fight the 'enemy' he'll fight us with his pens.

Brize Norton mourns another soul, another young man's life,
Another conflict far away. 'A necessary strife.'
Another suit, another face, another pudgy hand,
Who'll send us to our duty in another foreign land.

They talk with solemn countenance, theirs is a fiscal cost,
They balance what the war is worth against the soldiers lost,
I sit here in my rented flat and watch my small TV,
Just a casualty of war, another amputee.

A new war then develops, a war that no one sees,
A dirty war, those men with pen's 'fight me' behind the scenes.
Men who sit in lavish suits, 'the cats who get the cream,'
Men who'll cut my recompense and take my self esteem.

Dan Lake

The Crack of Dawn

As dawn peers round the corner where the mist is lying deep
the moon is disappearing from the sky,
as I listen I can hear the low whistle of a train,
above the noisy mallards flying high.
I reach and pull the covers up and wonder to myself
what fate decrees to greet this brand new day,
will I stay a moment longer, while musing in the warmth,
or rise to chase the cats with morning prey.

The moon has made its journey to the far side of the world
and stars have followed on within its sight,
while deep within my garden walls I've heard the echoes call,
as wild things stalk their victims through the night.
I see the chintzy curtains waver in the morning breeze
and wonder if the larks are on the wing,
will I stay a moment longer, while musing in the warmth,
or rise to feed the blackbirds as they sing.

Though scarce ten minutes have now passed and here's the paperboy
he whistles as he turns into the lane,
I see the mist still floating and the street lamp shining through,
as I embrace my feather counterpane.
The day has dawned in glory for my blossoms to unfurl
where dragonflies will soar on wings of lace,
will I stay a moment longer, while musing in the warmth,
or turn to kiss my darling's handsome face.

Lulu Gee

Give me Respect

Give me the oceans
Give me the breeze
Give me the moonshine
Give me the trees
Give me your time
Give me a theme
But most of all darling
Please give me 'esteem'

Give me some sweetbread
Give me some wine
Give me some laughter
Give me your time
Give me your love
Give me your fire
But most of all darling
Please give me 'admire'

Give me forever
Give me your smile
Give me your friendship
Give me a mile
Give me your word
Give me effect
But most of all darling
Please give me 'respect'

Dan Lake

Sheets of White Linen

Sheets of crisp, cool linen as white as falling snow
Fragranced from love making just a little while ago,
When two hearts pulsated and ventured beyond time,
Searching for deep valleys yet high pinnacles to climb.

Sheets of crisp, cool linen as white as falling snow
Creased with love abandoned just a little while ago,
Hidden places softly kissed as sweet as honeydew,
Flew higher than the stars to a moonlit rendezvous.

Sheets of crisp, cool linen as white as falling snow
Covered moistened beads of flesh a little while ago,
While supple, pliant limbs yielded to each caress,
Desires were fulfilled with a masterly finesse.

Lulu Gee

Because Of You

You've given me resilience, I'll face the world head on,
I'll stand among the multitude and sing an awkward song,
I'll walk upon the stage of life and dance the night away;
Those things that age has tempered now seem worn and soft today
Because of you.

The cloak that once suppressed me is replaced by loving eyes,
The storm clouds that possessed me are replaced by sunny skies,
The fetters that restrained me are replaced by caring tones
My body is invigorated, strengthening these bones,
Because of you.

Where once I stood abandoned I now have you by my side,
When once my life was empty its repleted, satisfied,
My face was downcast; dutiful, a smile was just a smile
And now I'm full, resplendent, I will walk that extra mile,
Because of you…

Dan Lake

I Wish

I often wish that I could sail
To far off lands beyond the pale,
Instead of sitting here depressed,
No longer looking at my best.
I'd sail the oceans far and wide,
With silver moonbeams as my guide,
Transporting me to desert isles,
With no computers or mobiles.

I often wish that I could fly,
Just pack my bags and say goodbye,
Instead of listening to the news
And Gordon Brown's outrageous views.
I'd pilot my own private jet,
To fly to France for crepe suzette,
And guzzling pink champagne galore,
I'd buy French knickers from Dior.

I often wish that I could ski,
To simply wave my hand and flee,
Instead of sitting in the cold,
With global warming taking hold.
If I could ski down a black run,
I'd think I'd done the pools and won,
Such an exhilarating fear -
To ski a mountainside that's sheer.

I often wish that I could sing,
To swing the blues and sing like Bing,
Instead of miming to a tune,
When all I want to do is croon.
If I could sing then I would dance,
In fishnet tights I'd kick and prance,
Wearing a sequinned leotard,
I'd take the stage and promenade.

I used to wish that I were dead
And free from mortal fear and dread,
To free myself from stress and strains,
But then I don't have many brains.
But now I'm happy as a lamb,
'Frankly my dear, don't give a damn,'
As long as I can see springtime,
To make my verses flow with rhyme!

Lulu Gee

Her Tom

She rises in the morning and she stretches her lithe form,
He lies beside her so content, battle scarred and worn,
But she's no inclination to allow him the more rests
And slowly lifts her arm up high exposing her firm breasts.

She straddles him before he wakes and slowly moves her hips
To a slow tune she's forgotten, then she feels her own moist lips,
Then seeing this old Tom beneath her, passion for him dies
And rolls off to enjoy the pool, of passion 'twixt her thighs.

She closed those eyes of emerald green and saw another man,
One of power, an Indian, Apache or Cheyenne.
A great bronze man of energy who'd fulfil her desires,
Who'd satisfy her every thought and long put out her fires.

Her body heaved her mouth groaned words no one would ever know,
Her fingers showed him where to please; his lips knew where to go
And while she rode this buckskin man who made her moan and
weep,
Her Tom snored long beside her as he too enjoyed his sleep.

Dan Lake

Something

Something has happened to my heart, it seems to beat so fast
And look, the spell has lifted now that made me sad, downcast,
For I can hear a voice so soft that makes my blood run warm,
As sure as raindrops gently fall and rainbows soft perform.

At last the road is not so long and lonely, for I see
The beauty that I never saw when there was only me.
It seems a bouquet from a rose can linger in the air,
If placed into a treasured vase arranged with loving care.

Something has happened to my heart, for only yesterday,
I saved a spider from sure death and sent him on his way
And suddenly I'm not afraid of shadows hiding there,
I only see such lovely things around me, everywhere.

As now I hear the blackbirds sing with joy in mist at dawn,
When from my slumbered rest I wake to greet the early morn.
At times the grey clouds kiss the sun but they will surely pass,
Just like the spell of misery that followed me first class.

Something has happened to my heart, for love has come to me,
It's late I know but swiftly came with magic chemistry
And as the moon is held aloft by heavens east and west,
I've memories within my palm to hold upon my breast.

Something has happened ....

Lulu Gee

The Noise of Nonsense

Have you heard the silence in my cold and white domain,
It's as loud as a tornado or a speeding express train,
I can't hear myself for thinking
For the ructions in my brain,
In the evening of my winter wonderland.

The snow falls with the thunder of a mighty avalanche,
Defying even gravity upon the thinnest branch
And wipe the colour from the land
Like an etiolate blanch,
In the evening of my winter wonderland.

I'm deafened by the snoring of the field-mouse in his nest
As I lay awake at night and hear the pounding in my chest,
Obsessed with pandemonium
I have become depressed,
In the evening of my winter wonderland.

Dan Lake

Precious Hours

They lie here on their perfect day beneath ivory sheets,
So happy for the world to pass them by,
She looks into his sapphire eyes and hears her own heartbeats
And suddenly she feels a need to sigh.

Contentment overwhelms her as they lay in perfect bliss,
His fingers gently stroking her warm skin,
These precious hours are stolen for an afternoon like this,
Away from household stress and bank admin.

Her hair is loose and freshly washed, floating across his chest,
Like silken threads to softly tantalise,
With kisses soft as angel's wings she tells him he's the best
And seeks his lips so soft to emphasise.

As lovers do, they lie here quite oblivious to all,
Each kiss has sailed them to a far off land,
She's climbed the highest alp and he's seen tigers in Bengal
And heard the jazz ring out in Dixieland.

For many years they've come each month to stay at this hotel,
Meeting as if strangers every time,
She wears her finest lingerie and scents for him to smell
And from the bar they drink a gin and lime.

The sunlight is now sinking so they know the time has come,
To rise up from these sheets of ivory,
Returning to their lives until the next time they succumb,
To precious hours of impropriety.

He pays for the hotel room and they stand in soft twilight,
She smiles into his face so warmly tanned,
It's then she takes his hand in hers and sighs, 'see you tonight,'
For twenty years he's been her dear husband!!

Lulu Gee

As Good As It Gets

I looked inside a heart today and saw a caring face,
A smile, a love for mankind and received a warm embrace.
Though weary through a journey that should leave repugn or mar
There's no sign of disenchantment, open wounds or any scar.
No countenance of bitterness though suffered so much pain,
But a soft and gentle heart within so full of sweet refrain.
This heart lies down for others never measuring the cost,
It's arms embrace all humankind not counting what's been lost,
A brave-heart filled with fortitude from sun-up to sunsets,
It cries and laughs for everyone; It's as good as it gets…

Dan Lake

Elgar's Storm

'Land of Hope and Glory,' marches with the storm,
Startling the willows and threatening the haulm,
Amusing gales with cornets sweet,
Denying not the bass drum's beat,
As on this gusty night they all perform.

Buds anew are mourning as the rain blows cold,
Lapping at my roses, silky pink and gold,
While trembly violins pluck low,
To match the harp's melodious flow
As trumpets sound and rivers swell threefold.

Thunder cracks on impulse higher than the sky,
Breathing oh so heavy trying to race by,
Presaging, as a clarinet
Crescendos with the salicet,
Bewildered by storm demons up on high.

With fear this windy, sleepless night surrounds me,
As terns are trying to flee the squalls at sea,
Then bass bassoons and oboes sound,
As piccolos and flutes astound
The waves that over-ride the rasping quay.

Far below horizons where the sun's long set,
Gulls and waves on chargers roar their own duet,
As cymbals crash upon seashells,
Three triangles add decibels
Beneath the stars and moon's own silhouette.

Still wailing is the wind whipping like a sail,
Shrieking like a tempest mid the bitter hail,
Enraged with pomp and circumstance,
Yet marching in a rhythmic stance
As promenaders encore and regale.

Clouds with pennons streaming dance a fine chasse,
As the side drum's tapping, echoes o'er the bay,
With sweeping highs and lows of wind
And trumpets blasting determined,
Ten thousand voices sing the storm away.

Lulu Gee

The Final Blow

The warrior sank to his knees
His pulse is beating slow,
His words fall silent on the breeze
His eyes no longer glow.
His life is failing, quick to part
His breath it comes in gasps,
No longer strong this prince's heart,
Inaudibly he rasps.

No gore runs from his broken shell
His scars are old and aged,
Many times he's fought through hell
While bloodied, torn, enraged.
But we can't see this battlefield
More powerful than life.
The final blow that makes him yield
Is losing his sweet wife.

Dan Lake

Rime Mountain

The snow clouds swirl around my head and all the world is ice,
oh, if only you were here this could be paradise.
Beside the mountainside it's still and quiet as the grave,
with only tears from icicles in this my barren cave.

The snow clouds swirl like gauzy veils upon this cheerless day,
each cloud marbled a raspberry pink like an iced parfait.
Oh, what has happened in my heart, I cannot find the words,
not even to the mountain sheep or dawn awakened birds.

The snow clouds swirl in splendour as I smell the edelweiss,
so tender in a vase now, the mountain's sacrifice.
I feel the spell is lifting that has made my blood run cold;
the magic castle is in view, a talisman in gold.

The snow clouds swirl and slumber as I scale the icy piste;
the castle swings open its doors bestowing me a feast.
At last the tide is turning and true love will take its course,
as sure as moonbeams shimmering upon the winter gorse.

The snow clouds swirl but now I feel the kissing of the sun
and hark, a thousand songbirds, in chorus every one.
No longer do I see the cave below the clouds that swirl,
now all I see are twinkling stars in silver, gold and pearl.

Lulu Gee

The Prodigal Returns

What lies beyond yon door that's swinging free,
Should I enter, should I wander in,
The door is open, but ajar for me!
Why do I feel I've staged a mortal sin?

I need to look beyond but can't engage,
My hand won't reach to touch I'm so afraid.
I'm looking in but have no way to gauge,
The darkness lying past looks dead, decayed.

Who waits beyond the pall, who do I hear,
Why tempt me with admission, should I see,
Is something there that I should truly fear
That sits in sentinel, the feared chargee?

Perspiration runs into my eyes,
I hear a voice, it chokes, like a disease,
I look up to the cloudless sunlit skies
And back again to feel my body freeze.

The door is opening, it's live I fear,
Slowly swinging wide to test, allure,
My feet are moving inch-meal ever near,
I can't control my legs, I'm so unsure.

I feel the blood seep from my pumping heart,
My mouth cries out but cannot make a sound,
My stomach feels as though it's ripped apart,
I stepped across the threshold homeward bound.

Dan Lake

Where Love Abounds

Where love abounds within my mind
It beats content, blissful, consigned,
Conveying all that love may bring,
For that soft heart that makes me sing
To one so sweet and so resigned.

The weightlessness of life entwined,
When beads of sweat become moon-shined
As heaven moves within the soul,
A cry, a joy to sweet console,
Where love abounds.

That afterglow, that sweet refrain
Within confines of our domain.
The silent smile, the softest kiss
That emanates from times as this,
A sensuous drink of life's champagne,
Where love abounds.

Dan Lake

Total Disarray

The sea looks calm today;
Much like my pensive vein,
For I'm left once again
With a grave and troubled low.
Beneath the gentle spray
A current strong, aflow,
That causes endless pain
As I'm hiding my dismay.

Why can't my heart display,
Why does it try to feign
And show I'm quite insane
In the waters deep below.
There's total disarray
On my aqueous plateau,
So fear I must explain
I'm not quite who I portray.

Dan Lake

Reconcile

She had not meant to fall asleep,
Only to rest a little while,
For over hill and golden vale
She'd walked with hopes of reconcile.

Towards the stream with slender ferns
That flows so silent in the shade,
And through the pine trees in between
The little churchyard in the glade.

Beyond was beach with yellow sand
Where foaming crests roll to the shore,
With shells of pink and purple hues
And gulls and terns in loud rapport.

She ran to meet the water's edge,
Her eyes amist with falling tears
And as the ocean called to her
She thought of all the wasted years.

She thought of gazing in his eyes,
When happiness was theirs to share
And as he kissed her curving lips
She'd float on clouds above the air.

The ocean stroked her gleaming throat
As once again she felt his breath
And felt his love envelop her,
As real to her as her own death.

She saw the church come into view
With sombre peals for evensong
And then the stream awash with life,
Had she been gone the whole day long?

She had not meant to fall asleep,
Only to rest a little while
For over hill and golden vale,
He brought her home to reconcile.

Lulu Gee

Resignation (sonnet)

I missed the world today (but I don't care),
It's raining and my mood has lost its way.
It's lonely here, with no-one else to share,
My hopes and fears, my thoughts from day to day.
The telephone is silent, (I don't mind),
When it rings it only brings me sorrow;
I wonder if beyond the veil I'll find,
Somewhere I might love my long tomorrow.
I hear a sigh that breaks the silent pall,
I listen, there is no-one, it was me,
Death rests on me as like a silent shawl
And opens up these doors to set me free.

This misery lies heavy in this room
Its physical, a dead and wasted womb.

Dan Lake

A Lonely Sigh

Loneliness is not a word to ponder;
your mind can play all sorts of funny games,
coercing you to places you don't care for,
where sense and rationale go up in flames.

A wise man thinks he knows beyond despair,
but loneliness breeds doubt alongside fears,
when no-one shares our love or happiness,
We can but only cry sad, lonely tears

To share a joy with someone else awhile,
or feel a touch that says, I still love you,
or hear a voice that speaks of reassurance,
when holding you with love the whole night through.

Friends say, 'farewell, it's been so nice to see you,'
but once the door has closed upon them all,
four walls close in to meet the dying embers,
the only sound is time and your footfall.

Lulu Gee

Those Eyes (Octet)

If we could just but see
Who hides behind the eyes,
Those come on in for free
Inviting window panes.
Are you enticing me
With metronomic lies,
Or am I all at sea
With caution in my veins.

I look but can't attain
The answers I pursue.
I'm outside my domain,
I fear the baited snare.
Those eyes say I'm insane,
There's nothing to construe,
I'll never ascertain,
I haven't got a prayer.

Those eyes that stole my mind:
I beg them to be kind…

Dan Lake

A Life No More

My past life is but mine no more,
It's ravaged to the inner core.
The years and hours are almost gone,
In flames, a veil of fine chiffon.

Alone I stand with tearful eyes,
Afraid to lift them to the skies,
Anguish with pains tear at my soul,
As for my life I take control.

Whatever will become of me?
I cry and clasp my hands to plea,
So old to start my life anew,
To seek new love forever true.

If by a miracle I find,
A heart with vows to fill my mind,
I'll toil each second and some more,
To fit the last piece of jigsaw.

Lulu Gee

The Rendezvous

She stood there on the Esplanade
Where they had met so long ago,
The pier was bright its lights aglow;
Her recall often made her smile.

She'd been so late, a country mile,
He'd smiled and said he didn't care,
So long ago when they met there
And strolled along the Promenade.

Every year that trip he made
So now she waited patiently,
She knew that he would come; she'd see
That glowing smile, that innocence.

Appearing by some transience
As he had done so many times,
At eight o'clock the church bell chimes
His timing set her heart aglow.

He took her arm; he was her beau
While teasing her they strolled along,
The moon above, the gas lamps shone,
On rowing boats and strong oarsmen.

Some sixty years had passed since then,
Some sixty years had come and gone
Since she had died, it seemed so wrong,
That night the pier went up in flames.

He'd kept that rendezvous each year
Not knowing that she waited near,
He'd never wed, he'd never kissed,
Still aching for the love he missed.

Dan Lake

Lapin a La Cocotte (Rabbit Stew)

Today, this very afternoon
The sun looks down with warmth to spare,
From scented skies with good fortune
Into my pleasant kitchen, where
I'm slow cooking a new caught hare.

Into my cast iron casserole
I pour more wine than is desired,
Then add the veg to slowly boil,
With rousing smells to be admired
And juicy taste buds fresh afired.

I just have time to take a nap
Before the night draws still and sweet,
Before the cat jumps on my lap,
With taloned claws that pad so fleet
And mind of mischief and conceit.

She takes possession absolute
As on my lap she's proud and lone,
I won't argue, there's no dispute
My home's no longer quite my own
And so I nap as her purrs drone.

Its twilight now and so I dress
Leaving my shoulders smoothly bare,
Just as the moon starts to caress
My freckled skin, my loosened hair,
Attracting his approving stare.

With finery the table's laid,
Reflecting crystal in my eyes,
Beneath the stars and pines of jade
Where all is lit by fireflies,
For shadows dark are drawing sighs.

The curlew's wail is drifting high,
Over the flame of candle light
As owls are flying by and by
And in between each morsel bite,
A stolen kiss this special night.

And later when I'm in his arms
I know I'll nestle safe and deep,
With no concerns or nightmare qualms
In afterglow I'll sigh and weep,
Then like a child .... I'll fall asleep.

Lulu Gee

No Rhyme, No Reason

He sits with head in hands and groans,
His attributes picked to the bones
By those monosyllabic crones who mock him.

He loses will, he can't compete,
Graffiti written in the street,
In text like language, incomplete, defeats him.

Who taught these children, heaven knows,
To write in base generic prose,
Failed teachers one can just suppose, it haunts him.

To him it seems an awful crime,
To teach that prose can conquer rhyme,
Meter and form aren't worth a dime,
Syllable count that keeps the time,
Those rules of stress, (to him sublime,)
Are worthless garbage, now't but grime, dejects him.

Dan Lake

One Heartbeat

When she met him at the station it was almost half past ten,
She knew for her steps echoed to the sounds of old Big Ben.
With smiles to light up London and a kiss to start a fire,
His eyes were singing melodies that echoed with desire.
Then holding hands they escalated from the subway's heat,
So happy and in love with breaths of one heartbeat.

They strolled in bliss to Marble Arch through flurries of soft snow,
With tender love they should have found so many lives ago
And all the time he squeezed her hand to keep her by his side,
Hoping perhaps one day she would consent to be his bride,
Whereby their lives could start again and once more be complete,
So happy and in love with breaths of one heartbeat.

At twilight beneath city lamps it seemed the world was kissed,
By frosty shadows flickering aswirl in London's mist.
They ate cuisine in China Town and laughed the whole meal through,
Then slowly took the underground for trains at Waterloo -
Where weeping tears they said farewell with kisses honey sweet,
So happy and in love with breaths of one heartbeat.

Lulu Gee

Oh Mystic Beast. (My latent muse)

Some mystic beast lies dormant
within my ageless soul.
It walks with me, becalmed and still
exerting no control.
What stirs its flame without the norm
of love, or pain and fear,
then brings it forth to prompt my soul
and write, I've no idea.

I can't begin to tell you now
of places I have been;
amongst the mundane wheels of life
that mystic beast will glean,
some reverent inspiration,
some feint within its glen;
that makes it rise as if sunrise
then dares me lift my pen.

Oh mystic beast within my heart,
allow me mastery.
Permit my thoughts to provoke you,
delight occasionally.
I ask not for your servile grace
or steal your jeu d'esprit;
I ask you to release my muse
and restore life to me…

Dan Lake

A Day Trip

The train to Brighton town moved slow
but when two miles away,
I saw the Downs and then the sea
with white horses at play.
Beneath an unencumbered sky
the panting train rolled free,
through patterned fields and curving hills
each beckoning to me.

The sea gulls cried with happy tunes
above our whistling train,
for dancing was the southern breeze
with neither mist nor rain.
The air was crystal, sweet and clear
with not a cloud to shade,
only a lovely azure sky
over a sea of jade.

We sauntered through the antique shops
that lined the cobbled lanes,
discussing everything we saw
from guns to antique canes
and everywhere we seemed to go
we glimpsed the wondrous sight,
of Brighton's Royal Pavilion
aglow for our delight.

Then like a jewel was Brighton's prom,
above the waterline,
standing before the pebbled beach
that glistened in the brine
and as we stood entwined with love
we vowed to come back soon,
to step into The Grand Hotel
for tea, one afternoon.

Lulu Gee

The Power of the Word Love.

I found a word I think I must enhance,
An anaphor with soul where dreams are made,
The use of which can make you sing or dance,
Appearing often in a serenade.

When breathed indifferently from sultry lips,
Or whispered through the tears of knavish pain,
Those charlatans steal from the cup with sips,
Deceiving, seeking which they might attain.

But those of us who dream beyond the day,
Who look into the eyes that soft impart,
While hearing someone special softly say,
Will keep that ruby ever in our heart.

Then while we breathe we feel that gem evolve,
And face the world with courage and resolve.

Dan Lake

A Christmas Tale

‘Tis the week before Christmas and all is not well,
There’s a pause in Santa’s supplies,
In attempting to satisfy young clientele,
He’s moaning and groaning with sighs.

There are gnomes making toys with six naughty green elves,
The Polar Bear manages them,
But they’re on a go slow lazing round on the shelves,
It’s causing chaos and mayhem.

The Polar Bear bellows ‘til gravelly and hoarse,
But elves giggle loud in his face.
They disputingly clash as a matter of course,
Refusing to step up their pace.

Wilhamine the Cockhorse enters in the affray,
Appealing to cease this mischief,
With a whirl and a swirl, she rears up with a neigh
Flinging high her spotty kerchief.

The assembly line stops in the midst of this brawl,
Leaving Santa shaking with rage,
For there’s not a toy soldier, a doll or a ball,
Or picture books showing a page.

With a red nose, Rudolph saw this hullabaloo
Deciding ‘disgracing’ be done,
Saying, ‘scolding from squabbling is long overdue
For Christmas should replicate fun.’

He showed each the lists that some children had sent him,
Ill-fated with hardships and drought,
Wanting Christmassy bears tied with blue ribbon trim,
‘Do you want to see them go without?’

Now the elves shake their heads in both shame and remorse,
Agreeing to resume their work,
And The Polar Bear asks Wilhamine The Cockhorse,
To make sure they’ll no longer shirk.

Now ‘tis late Christmas Eve and all are delighted,
The sleighs heavy laden with gifts.
With farewells and cries of, ‘Rudolph make it snappy,
Take care over icy snowdrifts.’

Rudolph escorts Vixen and Dasher and Dancer,
With Comet and Blitzen as well.
And to bring up the rear is Donner with Prancer,
Insisting he wears a new bell.

Through the star spangled night when we’re all fast asleep,
Santa quietly creeps to each house,
To leave all that you wish in a tinsel tied heap,
Then Shhhh! .... Leaves as quiet as a mouse.

Lulu Gee

The Abyss

They walked as they had done before, those cliffs of pure delight,
Hand in hand they'd strolled among the moon and stars at night,
Secure in their own company, so safe within their world,
She never saw the thief approach or what could have unfurled.

The night she slipped from love's embrace his heart recoiled in fear,
The danger far below evoked a feeling so severe.
Shocked by the beguiler and confronted by alarm,
While stumbling back in disbelief her lover grasped her arm.

She fell, he held her perilous, he feared the rocks below,
He cried, 'please take my hand my love,' grasping from his plateau,
She swung below in the abyss, he feared his love was gone
And as the footpad slipped away he desperately held on.

She feared that he would also fall, she begged him let her go,
With tears that fell on her sweet face he angrily cried, 'no
My love I'll never let you go, now grasp my other hand,
Before we both fall on the rocks and spill blood on the sand.'

She reached with trepidation as she grasped his outstretched palm,
She felt the strength she'd known before start hauling her from harm,
Determined now to rid herself of terrors in her chest,
He hauled her from the chasm to the safety on the crest.

The moon and stars still glittered as they held each so secure,
They knew now there was nothing in this world they won't endure.
They kissed their tears from weeping eyes and pledged the lord above,
That nothing earthly could divide their loyalty and their love.

And one day in their dotage they will share this memory,
That gave them strength to life itself until eternity.

Dan Lake

Meanderings in Madness

Don't look my way I seek perfection!
But my mind's no recollection
Of the words that make you laugh or make you cry.
I fear the outward motion
That denies the words promotion
As you sit and read my script and wonder why.
You have no understanding
Of the fear of my mishandling
Of a subject that's so conscious in my mind,
But if I was just able
To lay words upon the table
Then you'd think I'm smart, an academic kind.

But I'm no academic
Though I know it's just endemic,
Of thoughts that go on with my complement.
We try to form a motion,
A wide rock and rolling ocean
That's little understood but warmly sent.
Our secrets are on paper
Or floating around like vapour
Like the food called words we fear we can't supply.
It's a form of dire starvation
In my struggle for creation
Just like Michael in the fields of Athenry.

Dan Lake

I Bought Myself a Satnav

My map-reading is terrible; my husband told me so,
as on one summer's day we planned a journey to Hounslow,
he barked, 'it's upside down Lu, oh bloody hell we're lost
can't you navigate this outing before November's frost?'

So today I bought a Satnav to help me plot a course
at getting me around more after break-up and divorce,
I'll venture further than before without my husband's crap,
without his yelling, snarling voice that came without gift-wrap,

For now I've got my 'Derek' and he guides me from above,
to steer me with His satellites, who knows, I might find love!
I turn the car's ignition and I hear Him say, 'turn round,'
in his attractive, soothing tone he tells me where I'm bound.

His voice is dark and sexy, never cross or out of sorts,
He never farts or picks his nose and never ever snorts,
I bet if I could see him, I would love him at first sight -
this Satnav I call 'Derek,' my polite and shining knight.

He tells me to go left or right or round the roundabout
and should I miss a turning He will never ever shout,
politely He says, 'turn around and take the next exit,'
I couldn't be without Him, as we steer the earth's orbit.

Lulu Gee

That Lie

Oh what tangled webs we weave,
From tiny lies there's no reprieve,
From lie on lies grow angry verse
Causing much pain and vulgar curse,
Until the lie yourself believed;
But now in loneliness bereaved.

From humble outsets serpents grow,
Innocent enough, although
You wonder why that first white lie,
Should lead to such a hue and cry
Encapsulates yon body blow,
That bends and brakes that weakened bow.

That spring once strong has lost its dream
Lies broken in its own esteem,
Irreparable, it's done,
No more the innocence or fun,
No more the eyes of truth agleam;
No more to stand and self redeem.

No more the trust on every word
That lie, the obvious, absurd.

Dan Lake

The Fisherman

A man I know went fishing to catch but only roach,
  not a bream and a not a pike nor salmon to encroach.
He sat all day a fishing with rods and bait of bread,
  maggots, hemp and casters quite near to Maidenhead.

The roach were there and biting, his waggler told him so,
  bobbing on the surface as the roach swam to and fro.
With shining flanks of silver and fins of ruby red,
  like submarines patrolling the murky river-bed.

Bait was seized and eaten while floats ducked all a dither,
  as a roach as big as him took a biting slither.
Such a struggle was enforced upon that riverbank,
  where the air was blue with rage and all the coffee drank.

And as the roach and fisherman fought into the night,
  their labouring commotion crept into dawn's first light.
They thrashed 'til all the river fizzed like a pink champagne,
  but it would not be landed, alas not this campaign.

With a mighty flying leap the fish made his escape,
  leaving that poor fisherman in shock with mouth agape.
He knew when he was beaten so packed up for the day,
  to tell all who would listen of ... the one that got away!!

Lulu Gee

Sweet Innocence

Sweet innocence of life you scheme
To see the world through grownup eyes,
I tell you now there's no surprise,
About those things we dare to dream.

You're growing now, my how you change,
The dolls have gone, the dreams diverse
You use your wiles, you're not averse
To falsify or rearrange.

How present have your dreams aspired,
A fantasy, a young pop star
With tight jeans and a super-car,
Those other girls have so admired.

Pregnancy! You have no cash,
The car has gone along with dreams,
He sits and plans his failing schemes
The tag has landed, 'trailer trash.'

The handout cheque arrives at last,
Three children and he's run away,
You drink some more to ease your day,
Could this have been pre-planned, forecast?

The knock comes on the trailer door
Through bleary eyes you try to smile,
No adverse thinking cunning guile,
At twenty one a sottish whore.

Sweet innocence of life you schemed
And now you see through grown up eyes,
You see it now there's no surprise,
About those things we dared to dream.

Dan Lake

I Have Love (Triolet)

I feel your kiss against my own
And sigh with wonder at your touch,
You smell divine with musk cologne,
I feel your kiss against my own.
No longer must I stand alone
For I have love within my clutch,
I feel your kiss against my own
And sigh with wonder at your touch.

Lulu Gee

I See You Everywhere (Triolet)

I see you everywhere I look
And in each love song I revere
In magazine and story book
I see you everywhere I look
In each and every crannied nook
Your face is smiling crystal clear
I see you everywhere I look
And in each love song I revere

Lulu Gee

The World That I Can't Defend

Will humanity spare a thought for me,
Or the care of a fragile rose,
Or the butterfly that will slowly die
As it beats at the grimed windows,
While the trams perspire in the loathsome choir
That's the voice of the outside's din,
The neon lights of the world's delights
Assault my world within.

Invaded dreams by the endless screams
Of the wail from the night's banshees,
As the black and whites cruise the endless nights
To awaken whom they please.
In my lonely bed on a lonely street
In a lonely bruising town,
I take a slug of the amber drug
That has brought my small world down.

In the room above I can hear their love,
They're escaping the world I see,
While the row below seems to undergo
A script from world war three.
Our chiefs employ those that quick deploy
The swipe of a baton's kiss,
As our president seems to implement
More controls while we live like this.

Can I just once say how my sad today
Was rewarded with heinous dread,
On the dirty streets where the thieves compete
For the souls of the walking dead,
Where all I need is a smile indeed
To say that it's not the end,
Just a gentle kiss wouldn't go amiss
In this land of an absent friend.

Will someone see that it's only me
In a world that I can't defend.....

Dan Lake

Much Laughter in the Air

The restaurant was busy with much laughter in the air,
On the night they sat together in the 'Bistro Chanticleer.'
They had spent the day sightseeing, for this their first meeting
And now sought refuge for a meal as light was fast fading.
She told him over salmon mousse how she had lived her life,
Regaling him with anecdotes of happiness and strife.
He said he'd wished they'd met before when they were very young,
And stroked her arm so softly 'neath her jacket of shantung,
She knew that she could love this man with ev'ry waking hour,
And suddenly a nightingale woke in his leafy bower.

The restaurant was busy with much laughter in the air,
On the night they sat together in the 'Bistro Chanticleer.'
A dozen times they'd eaten here but still it felt the first,
And as he took her hand in his her heart felt it would burst.
He told her over entrecotes' how much she meant to him,
She was the air he breathed and his every working limb,
With not a moment passing that he didn't think of her,
She cried hot stinging tears and his face became a blur.
She knew though without seeing there was stardust in his eyes
And suddenly a nightingale looked at the moonlit skies.

The restaurant was busy with much laughter in the air,
On the night they sat together in the 'Bistro Chanticleer.'
A hundred times they'd eaten here and still he held her hand,
Still beautifully manicured but older now and tanned.
She told him over Torte Limone how happy she had been
And how her love was still as strong as all the years between.
They gazed out at the silver moon bedazzled by moonbeams
And thanked a million stars for fulfilling all their dreams.
The restaurant was busy with much laughter in the air,
When suddenly a nightingale sang for this grand affair.

Lulu Gee

The Leaf of Life

I sit by the windowsill watching the rain,
Rhythmically beating on my windowpane,
My eyes fill with tears as I look once again
At her face, as she smiles tenderly.

I call and I cry that she might reappear,
My darling, my angel that I'd held so dear,
That veil, that great mystery draws ever near,
The moment that she'll come for me.

My heart like the weather is windswept and cold,
My soul is departing I can't be consoled,
I'm empty and lifeless just like this household;
As the leaf that just clings to the tree.

Persistently battered alone in the gale,
It's just hanging on but it's withered and frail,
Then my grand finale, my final exhale;
The leaf fell and set my soul free.

Dan Lake

Memories

Beneath the sycamore she lies, her head resting on him,
above his voice wings swoop without a care,
while stars are at their best, dressed by the honey coloured moon,
as fireflies are dancing everywhere.

An ancient castle stands aloft beyond the Southern Downs,
as they recall a holiday spent there,
In autumn as the leaves turned gold and loveliness was theirs,
while fireflies were dancing everywhere.

A shadow plays about their feet as wispy clouds arrive,
to cast a glint upon his silvery hair,
while memories of times now shared are softly brought to mind,
the fireflies are dancing everywhere.

Meanwhile she's lost in happiness feeling the sweetest kiss,
from lips that are as soft as maidenhair,
just as the moon dips closer to enchant the atmosphere
the fireflies are dancing everywhere.

As sure as springtime comes around to start another year
and all of nature is *extraordinaire*,
their love for one another will shine brightly, for you'll see
the fireflies still dancing everywhere.

Lulu Gee

His Beautiful Princess

He watched, eyes staring downwards
In the warmly lit bedroom,
And saw the passions played below
Between the bride and groom,
Their eagerness to please and sate
Their own beguiled express,
Was tempered just enough to hide
Behind the tenderness.

The play performed a thousand times,
She'd act the part, serene,
But needed him to open doors
To places dark, unseen.
He laughed a silent salience
He'd seen it all before
The trousers, dress and stockings
All bedecked upon the floor.

He tired of all the dalliance
He wanted love, noblesse,
A hundred years he'd waited,
Just to see his real princess.
Then though his eyes were open
He was wakened from his gloom:
As his vision of pure loveliness
Appeared into his room.

His wooden heart appeared to move
He had no breath to hold,
His countenance was ugly and
His gesso'd face was gold,
But when she glanced upon him
She at once began to smile,
A warmness that began to melt
This half man half reptile.

She stood before him innocent
He wanted to possess,
Nubile, soft and graceful
She disrobed with soft finesse.
But he's a carving on the bed,
He's made from ancient oak
And though his wings reached out for her
He's shackled to his yoke.

With beauty in her nakedness
She smiled a warm embrace,
Revealing tears upon his cheeks
She touched his aged face,
His cold heart warmed and almost beat
A state of acquiesce,
That night he slept with love erstwhile,
His beautiful princess.

Dan Lake

The Dream Tree

The dream tree sits atop the world
Beneath the sequinned moon,
That glistens in the velvet sky,
As smooth as a balloon
And twinkling stars dance in delight
To cast light on the tree,
Its branches bathing in the glow
So that our dreams may be.

The tree is guarded well you know
Because dreams are like gold,
A serpent coils around the trunk
And hisses at the bold.
While snowy owls on wings of love
And wood nymphs who enchant,
Try to convey our dreams desired,
Pleading the tree to grant.

The tree is shaken once a year
And dreams become stardust,
That's when the fairies of the land
Must cease their wanderlust.
They sort the dreams for happiness
And those to stay tight furled
And all the while the tree of dreams,
Still sits atop the world.

Lulu Gee

Repent At Leisure (sonnet)

He kneels bereft, a bent and broken man,
He had it all and paid the consequence,
The tears he cries were never in the plan,
The willpower has gone with confidence;
It burns his veins, the thoughts ravage his mind,
(The poisoned chalice tasted good to sip).
He's fallen from his heaven, love is blind,
she's drifted on, she's just a passing ship!
But then he feels that softness he'd once known,
Those arms that he has pained deflect despair.
He feels her golden tears mix with his own,
The love he almost lost still wants him there.

No more to seek or want forbidden pleasure,
The pain and awful cost. Repent at leisure.

Dan Lake

Love

They fell in love a while ago,
While eating in a small bistro,
Paella with a fine merlot
And then cointreau and then cointreau.

And when they kissed, it felt so right,
Beneath the moon glistening white,
To say they wished to re-unite,
Another night, another night.

Such memories they have to share,
Of lover's trysts without despair,
With walks through town and country air,
And all that's there and all that's there.

Now two full years have almost passed,
Some folk declared it wouldn't last,
But their love's stronger and steadfast,
The die is cast, the die is cast.

'One day,' they always seem to sigh,
While dreaming, gazing to the sky,
'We'll be together, you and I,
Before we die, before we die.'

Lulu Gee

St Peter & Doubting Thomas

While standing at the pearly gates, St Peter said to me,
'Hello Thomas, what's to do for you?'
I said, ' I'm not quite sure sir, but could you please explain,
Where I go and what's my chosen queue?'
'That's easy,' said St Peter with a wave of his large hand;
'Join your queue of work where ere it be.'
My trade's a Cabinet Maker, but prose I'm writing now,
So joined the line that declared 'poetry.'

I wasn't in a rush and wasn't going anywhere
So stood in turn to get my invite in,
But seated at the table was Will Wordsworth looking young
And there Lord Byron sat right next to him.

'What was your education?' Will Wordsworth asked of me,
'It seems you can't write anything at all,'
And Byron interjected 'if you weren't a Cambridge man,
How can you be a bard? It's shite you scrawl.'
Thomas Hardy tried to help, suggesting I be heard,
Explaining to them he himself had beat,
The education system that had tried to keep him down.
I left the queue; I won't join these poor sheep.

'Don't worry lads, I kid you not,' I answered easily.
I have another queue where I can wait,
Then sought the queue for carpenters, indentured as I am,
There's always other choices at the gate.

Was I surprised when getting to the front eventually,
There at the grandest desk sat Chippendale,
With Sheraton at his right hand and Hepplewhite to boot;
I slowly told these renowned men my tale.
'A maker of fine cabinets, I see you have some skill;
Indentured yes, but you can't come in here,
You're lowly and you have no style, you're just a working man;
Your education fails you I fear.'

So walking round those countless halls of peace and harmony,
I thought I'd ask St Peter what to do,
Explaining that I'd given up on occupations now.
He said, 'Thomas the answers here for you.'
In a voice that shook the holy ground he waved his shepherds crook
For silence in the first room that he chose,
Then asked the multitude if there was one among them there,
Who'd gained enjoyment from my humble prose.

'See Thomas there's your answer' said the wise man pointing where,
An arm was raised among the silent throng;
'If that one soul has gained some peace from written words of yours,
Those sceptics who have judged you must be wrong.
Don't doubt good Thomas, please return to those that judge your toil;
Go back and say St Peter won't agree;
If you could bring enjoyment with your words or with your plane,
To just one man, that's good enough for me.'

A man of wood, a man of words, to me it matters not,
The heart that brings enjoyment's all I see.

Dan Lake

We'll Starve!!!

I can't think where I've put my purse,
I've looked both high and low
and now my temper's getting worse,
I think you ought to know.
I cannot shop for tea tonight,
the fridge is bare with not a bite,
I cannot shop
I cannot shop
for milk and bread and Vegemite.

I can't think where I've put my purse,
I had it yesterday,
I swear and with my every curse,
I tremble with dismay.
Have I been robbed by some coke head,
last night while sleeping in my bed,
have I been robbed
have I been robbed
the problem is by now they've fled.

I can't think where I've put my purse,
my house is now a tip,
I'm feeling faintly quite perverse,
I think I've lost my grip.
I'll ring the cops in record time,
for them to solve this awful crime,
I'll ring the cops
I'll ring the cops
and tell them all in perfect rhyme.

Lulu Gee

The Chimney Sweep

With eyes that peer through soot and dust
And lungs so full, he'd start to cough,
Edward Townsend swept chimneys
For citizens, of Lowestoft.

As a child he romped with Joe,
Two kids at play, their world complete.
But then aged eight Joe took a job,
A poor linkboy who walked the street.

Apprenticed to a man of soot
Our Edward sought himself a trade,
At twelve years old he climbed the flues
To clear the waste the fires made.

His brush and rods, his tools of work,
With hessian tied round his knees,
From terrace, manor house or croft,
To old steam trains and factories.

A conscientious man, Edward,
He worked till dusk from dawn's first light
With wife and children to upkeep,
He'd not get home till past twilight.

Year on year his lungs grew worse
His children flown now from the coop,
Though stoic pride shone in his eyes
He knew he had the dreaded croup.

Edward Townsend lay in his bed,
Now breathing shallow, lungs congealed,
He dreamt of times he played with Joe,
Two barefoot kids in stream or field.

The townsfolk came to pay respects;
From gentry to the poor, send-off
Our humble chimney sweep who lies;
Beneath this sod in Lowestoft

Lulu Gee and Dan Lake

I'd Love to Dance (Triolet)

I'd love to dance with you tonight,
To feel your cheek against my own,
When silver moonbeams are in sight,
I'd love to dance with you tonight.
Before my hair becomes too white
And I forget the dreams I've known,
I'd love to dance with you tonight,
To feel your cheek against my own.

I'd love to dance within your arms,
In moon glow falling from the sky,
Feeling the magic of your charms,
I'd love to dance within your arms.
Maybe to Chopin, Liszt or Brahms
Before my time arrives to die,
I'd love to dance within your arms
In moon glow falling from the sky

I'd love to dance with you once more,
Just once before the fiddler flees,
Just once before the last encore,
I'd love to dance with you once more.
Maybe within the ocean's roar
Of her sweet calling harmonies,
I'd love to dance with you once more,
Just once before the fiddler flees.

Lulu Gee

The Organ Grinder

Who is the organ grinder; who creates the power?
Winding every year of every day of every hour,
Making every tiny key
That sits beneath the ebony
Rise and fall in harmony,
Who creates the power?

Who will choose the song to play, who changes the roll,
Who decides the music that will move the very soul?
Will my penny change the song
From classical to sing along,
Whose arm is it that seems so strong;
Who will change the roll?

Who will make the monkey dance, who will pull the string,
Who determines all! Who stands in silence, who will sing?
Has it all been planned, foretold,
Is no-one there we might behold,
Is serendipity condoled,
Who will pull the string?

Dan Lake

I Have a Rendezvous

At our appointed meeting place,
When snowdrops bathe in sun with grace,
Then in the garden I shall peep
To wake the dormouse from his sleep,
When hedgerows start to need a trim,
I have a rendezvous with him.

I hope that he will smile at me
And if he does I guarantee
My eyes will fill up to the brim,
Because I rendezvous with him,
I'll be enmeshed within his spell,
As if I'm on a caravel,
Sailing upon the seven seas
To far-off lands and colonies.

He'll take my hand and kiss my lips
And fill my head with funny quips
And I will nod and then I'll tease
And give his hand in mine a squeeze
And we'll declare our loves still true,
Thank God we kept this rendezvous.

Lulu Gee

The Poet's Box

It started on the workshop bench, a doodle with a pen,
Then measurements were taken and the whole thing drawn again,
Evolving slowly in my mind the seed began to grow,
Where thoughts became a firm idea where winds of dreams would blow.

Alter this then changing that, would that work from the plan,
'Ah yes if I change that to this, I think maybe it can,'
Drawings became timber from the altered cutting list
And notions became tangible, they started to exist.

Dovetails for the corners and the ash veneer inside,
Fitted with those secret drawers that gives a sense of pride,
Abraded with the finest grits and polished with shellac,
The insides were perfection now the outsides to attack.

A careful choice of burr veneer, it's from the London plane,
A tree walked past by millions who'd never know its name.
The finest woods shall dress this box, a rare and busy weave,
With boxwood for the stringing on the edge just to relieve.

With locks and fixtures fitted it's in glorious array,
That final touch of polish will complete its fine display;
And now the moment waited for, she takes it, so sincere,
A gasp, a smile, a gentle touch, a kiss and then a tear.

Dan Lake

Holding Hands

I walk with you in sunlight and I feel your fingertips,
While our footsteps hurry to our rendezvous,
I sense what you are thinking so on tiptoe kiss your lips
As your eyes say things I cannot misconstrue.
For our love is like the sunshine in the stainless blue of sky
Before descending twilight when the hunting owls drift by.

I walk with you in rainstorms and I feel your hand in mine
As a million clouds are cool and volatile,
Between us there's no distance as your arms with mine entwine,
And we pause to steal a kiss and softly smile.
For our love is like forget-me-nots in drifts upon the hill,
Before the summers ended and we feel the autumn's chill.

I walk with you at twilight as I feel you kiss my hand
While across the eastern skies the stars bestrewn,
Then watch an astral body falling from a silver strand,
As the lovely sleeping night surrounds the moon.
For our love is like a sapphire sea that laps the yellow sands,
Before our ship goes sailing on to many far-flung lands.

Lulu Gee

The Workshop

At last the time has come for him to close the workshop door,
The ghost of him still at his bench, odd shavings on the floor.
The planes and saws are packed away with chisels oiled and clean,
Waiting for another hand to start where his had been.

The stove now sits in quietude no more it burns his waste,
The scars on chops around the vice shows damage made in haste.
Spokeshaves that shaped cabrioles, fine saws that cut dovetails,
The rifflers used to carve his work are wrapped away with nails.

Who will use these many tools, show love and keep them keen,
Who will hold them firm of hand, make furniture or treen.
For fifty years he's used his tools, they'd been his friends nonstop,
For now, no more his hand would turn the key to his workshop!

Dan Lake

Miss Sissy Stork

Miss Sissy Stork was getting on
And every year or thereupon,
Her memory would have a lapse,
Was it old age? Well yes perhaps.
When young she flew both far and wide
Taking her orders from each bride,
With pen and pad she wrote it down,
A boy or girl and in which town
And sometimes quads and sometimes quins,
Or by demand just one or twins
And should the eyes be brown or blue,
With paler skin or darker hue.
By memory she got it right,
Delivering when dark or light
To house or flat or bungalow,
Miss Sissy Stork would always know.

But lately something's wholly lacked
For Sissy lost her way, in fact
Not once or twice but more I've heard,
She has become a wayward bird!
Each cloud now looks just like the rest
From Benidorm to Bucharest,
Through Canada and far Bombay
And all along the Milky Way,
The angels keep a watch on her
As Sissy's eyesight is a blur.
And so the angels bought a map
To help dear Sissy to recap,
Just where her babies need to be,
Which town, indeed which addressee,
For babies need to be on time,
Without mishaps or pantomime,

So Sissy with her glasses on
And map to hand can liaison,
Still taking orders from each bride
From everywhere both far and wide.
When Cupid takes a well earned rest
Sissy will do her very best
To babysit just for a while
And even though she's not agile,
She'll walk the babies through the park
Where birds will sing and dogs will bark
And trees will sway and stoop and bow,
When seeing Sissy Stork they'll sough,
Simply because they hold respect
For Sissy who with intellect
Will bring your baby, no delay,
Nine months from order, come what may!!

Lulu Gee

Veils of Soft Chiffon

Once I walked among you
Sharing smiles and shedding tears,
A touch, a word, those things we can't replace.
You look at happy photographs
Captured through the years,
That sit above your burning fireplace.

But I am not the flame that's burning
With a mortal source,
Manmade to be snuffed when need has gone.
Understand, for I am you
I have a divine course,
I'm here, beyond the veils of soft chiffon.

I shall never be erased,
I'll never be afraid,
Remember that I've simply gone away.
To live a time of quietude
Where I will never fade,
In peace and love, forever and a day.

Dan Lake

Dinner L'Amour

It's empty and late in the small bistro
and the maître d' is waiting to go,
but we've adjourned with a cafetiere,
into the garden with ripe camembert.

Our chateaubriand was cooked specially,
So was our hor d'oeuvre served with a Chablis
and everyone saw how in love we are,
as I shared with you my pear chocolat.

The candlelight flickers in the light breeze,
while magic's aloft high up in the trees,
then smiling you give my cheek a soft kiss,
as silky as dew in early morn mist.

We laugh about nothing as lovers do,
while under the moonlight's rich golden hue
and touching my shoulder, freckled and bare,
you kiss my warm lips, caressing my hair.

The moon scatters dreams upon this tableau
but the maître d' still wants us to go!!

Lulu Gee

A Day in Their Life

He's sitting barefoot on the step waiting for his dad,
Waiting as he's done so many times,
He smiled and said that all is well and 'no fings ain't too bad'
But I've learned I must read between the lines.

His tired smile and runny nose, his face devoid of love,
His skinny arms that grasp his bony knees,
His eyes have seen the evil of a life that doesn't care
As he shivers in the chilling winter breeze.

Another hungry face appears, scratching at his head
And tells me that his dad has, 'gone for grub,'
But I'd bet two to one that I know where their dads gone,
He's spending their food money in the pub.

'How's your mum,' I ask the itching tyke who needs a wash,
'She gorn to bed, she said that she ain't well.'
An answer that is so rehearsed it's said without a thought,
If true or not, I don't know, I can't tell.

I feel the tears well in my eyes, I want to take them home,
To bathe and dress them, feed them, watch them play.
Enjoy this time as other kids who live along this street,
Enjoying pleasures on this Christmas Day.

Dan Lake

The Fox

He stalks in silence dark as night,
Beneath the moon and breathless skies,
When black feathers are in full flight,
And all around are fearful cries,
As through the swathes of mist tonight,
He's guided by the fireflies.

He lies in wait by the lagoon,
His shadow in a pool of ink,
As crickets chant their sombre tune,
And in the distance eyes that blink,
As warm and golden as the moon,
They peer at him without a wink.

He plays his game of hide and seek
And suddenly with fearless heart,
He zig zags in a burnished streak,
To snare his quarry, not so smart,
Who was unwise to pip a squeak,
And make a feast of al a carte.

He can't dispute that life is sweet,
With all the craft and guile he's used,
For splendours that he's had to eat,
Without becoming harmed or bruised,
So with his appetite replete,
He sleeps in silence, quite bemused.

Lulu Gee

My Musical Princess

My tears fall on its Maple skin,
My heart is beating slow.
My memories come flooding back
From many years ago.
Those awkward shapes, those cutting strings,
My fingers pained and red,
But pain is nothing to a chord
Played well it's oft times said.

My shapely blonde accompanied me
Wherever I might bless,
Who ere I kissed I kissed again
My musical mistress,
We formed a band and roamed the land
Until some strange intone
Turned me against my sweet Hofner.
I bought an Epiphone!

My Hofner lay, just cast aside
No more did I caress,
That slender neck of strong rosewood
My musical princess;
But fornicated with strange notes
From new electric strings,
With amplifiers, copycats
And microphones and things.

I sold my cast off past mistress,
Virginal entente,
I thought me now a great master,
A learned swish savant,
But fifty years have passed since then,
Then one day from afar
A bag was left, with a short note;
'Dan, here's your old guitar.'

Dan Lake

The Legend of Pumpkin Jack

Old Pumpkin Jack on Halloween
starts kindly with a smile,
watching the children 'trick or treat,'
with happiness and guile.
But rapidly he tires of this,
he can't stay nice for long,
and soon his nasty side confirms
that Jack is still headstrong.

For when alive he tricked his way
with mean tight-fisted deeds,
and never seemed to care a jot
for other people's needs.
He tricked the Devil some do say
so he must pay the price,
and roam for all eternity
soulless, to be precise.

He's forced to wander in-between
Heaven and Devil's Hell;
for God won't let him in either
to join His clientele.
And so in darkness Jack must be
except for just one night,
when he's allowed a piece of coal
to flame his lantern light.

When thoughts of kindness seem to stray
the Devil sends in troops,
a Leprechaun with moles and warts
and whiskery beard that droops.
Then Demons who can fly like bats,
with horns that don't appeal,
while Pumpkin Jacks in miniature
wave swords to make him squeal.

Old Jack is screeched and bellowed at
and prodded here and there,
in fact he's trembly in his spats
with fear and cold despair!
The 'Trick and Treaters' MUST be scared,
insists the Leprechaun,
with screams and tricks of horridness
before tomorrows dawn.

So light your lantern Pumpkin Jack
and scare the gentle folk,
this night when spooky zombies haunt
and bats that shriek provoke,
in graveyards where ghouls dance on tombs
and skeletons arise,
as if by magic from the ground
before the next sunrise.

If you should see old Pumpkin Jack
the night of Halloween,
please don't be taken in by him,
his smile is a smoke-screen!!!

Lulu Gee

Dante's Nine Circles

I met God on a battlefield, worse than Dante's hell;
I told him I was so afraid, he said that he could tell.
We lay in limbo, bloodied for a thousand years or more
And he listened to me ramble as I talked of times of yore.

We lay together in that pit, that shell hole that was mine;
He held my head to comfort me until the end of time.
I opened up my life to him those things I must confess,
Then told him of my nine circles and this is my address.

My lust for girls excited me, I'd seduced them and lied,
I told him I was guilty of bedding my friend's bride,
I told him of voracity for food I'd never share,
I told him of my drunkenness and constant need to err.

I told him of my meanness, my excessive need for wealth,
How I could put my want for goods, before my mother's health!
I told him of my temper and how I'd just go crazy,
And how I wouldn't work because I'm negligent and lazy.

He knew of my apostasy, I'd turned my back on him,
I'd reached for failing doctrines, for no more than a whim,
I'd laid a hand on brothers with no care or thought for pain,
And kicked them to the floor so they would never rise again.

I'd grovelled in deception, so I'd cosset all I could
And played the game of treachery while mingling with the good.
Then crying in his arms I told him, I'd betrayed his love,
I'd laughed with Satan's minions and sneered at heaven above.

The battle raged above us as we lay there in the mud,
His khaki uniform was splattered with his holy blood,
He whispered don't be frightened this is where you're life begins,
And christened me with bloodied hand and forgave all my sins.

The bullets flew above us as my God said we must go,
He said that he would protect me, it's in the bible so
And wounded in his hands and feet, with barbed wire round his head,
He took my hand and led me to his world of peaceful dead.

Dan Lake

The Snowstorm

The soulless wind is streaming, across the plain its screaming,
  as with a trembling voice it heralds snow.
These fertile lands of goodwill, so hardened to the cold chill,
  are frozen deep where walking will be slow.

Silver clouds race ever high playing in a shrieking sky,
  as flurries start to gently kiss my face.
Quickly all is crystal white causing chaos at first light,
  where snowmen dressed for winter will embrace.

Now there's hardly any sound as snow cascades to the ground,
  only the crispy crunching from my feet.
So I'll linger for a while by the little wooden stile,
  to feel the storm as one with my heartbeat.

Darkened clouds of buttermilk smile at trees draped in white silk
  and the river is now silently inert.
You would think I'd hear a word from a workshy hidden bird,
  but storms are not the place for them to flirt.

No dark shadows here today, everything is ice frappe
  with wildlife staying warm in habitats.
For this winter storm is keen, it's the worst so far we've seen,
  and ladies are all wearing their fur hats.

Lulu Gee

Silent ships

I read your words, that one short line,
That's treasured in this heart of mine,
I hold your letter to my lips
While feeling your soft fingertips,
Then smell your perfume so sublime.

The grey day turns to soft sunshine
As you appear, then slow recline
In meadow grass and sweet cowslips,
I read your words.

I close my eyes to safe confine,
As tendrils from my heart entwine
You as we pass, like silent ships,
Then nothing can this world eclipse
The thought of you, so soft, divine,
I read your words.

Dan Lake

Blind Date

Upon the day she met him there were people passing by,
all going who knows where without a smile.
While waiting on the station, introverted and quite shy
she searched in every face at the turnstile.

The seconds turned to minutes as she wondered should she go,
was this a great mistake she would regret?
As trains were hissing wildly she then heard a whistle blow,
maybe she ought to wait a while... and yet.

It was then she saw him through a veil of shining tears,
a mirage in soft undulating sand,
But as he walked towards her he washed away the years
and smiling broadly held my soft, warm hand.

She'd never heard a birdsong until the day they met
nor seen a flame of autumn on a tree.
But here she was eyes gleaming, dancing a pirouette
and feeling liberated and carefree.

Since then each day is summer and all the world is warm
and kissing is in season all the year.
Today her heart's a mountainside, free of rains that storm,
as she ascends no longer does she fear.

Lulu Gee

Wined and Dined

She sat there on the floor napping
The 'I can't think syndrome.'
We'd been out celebrating
But at last we'd gotten home.
She'd relaxed talking to her friend
The big white telephone,
But was clinging on real tightly
Like a dog holding a bone.

She looked just like an angel
Who'd had just too much to drink.
I'd fed the dogs and washed the dishes
Lying in the sink,
Then while I'd turned the TV on
And watched the 'Missing Link,'
The house had gone real quiet
And I knew (she's out of sync.)

I found her in the bathroom
Quite demure but snoozing deep.
I picked her up and held her
And I prayed her soul to keep,
Then carried my sweet cargo
Up the stairs that were so steep,
Then kissing her goodnight
I left my angel there to sleep.

The memory of our night out will
Be etched firm in my mind,
We'd laughed and drank the night away,
We'd truly… wined and dined.

Dan Lake

Below Par

Why does today seem far away,
It hovers out of reach,
My soul seems dead like cold grey lead
As barren as my speech.

From mists of pearl that gently swirl
Around my aching head,
The hours unfold so uncontrolled
Are filling me with dread.

Such loneliness for a caress
Brings to my eye a tear,
To spill upon like fine chiffon
My heartache so severe.

But then I see a galaxy
Of beauty in the night,
A shining moon to make me swoon
And dance for his delight.

Lulu Gee

Carpets to Excite

A pirouetting princess fills her mind,
She saw her walking tall with perfect style,
Her chasse with her feet perfect aligned,
She'd curtsey just to see her mother smile.

Those memories faded as the car drew near,
She saw the driver look her up and down,
Tired and cold she smiled now through the fear
Then saw him drive off heading for downtown.

The dragon must be fed she felt the pain,
Her bony body ached for heroin,
Here comes another car, she'd try again,
He stopped, the door opened and she got in.

Her body used, her trick had dropped her back,
She hadn't got enough to fill her vein,
Should she go and score some cheaper crack,
Or try to get another trick again?

In headlights she appeared, a mannequin,
Disjointed and surreal in the moonlight.
Once she'd enjoyed famous mandarins'
Fat men with power taking her delight.

She'd stepped out on the carpets to excite,
In evening gowns of sequined silk so fine,
No feeling of remorse or cold contrite.
No thought to how her world could just decline.

How did this happen? How the puissant fell,
So quickly down the stairs from seeds she'd sowed.
Another car, another tortured hell,
She drove off with her saviour…down the road.

Dan Lake

The Raging Storm

Storm clouds are now raging at my window,
This dark, cold night I sit here all alone,
  Within me I feel fear
  Seeing shapes that aren't quite clear,
While listening to branches break and groan.

I will not close my eyes this blust'ry night,
As from the purple skies the winds vibrate,
  Creating tears and wrath
  For all that's standing in her path,
Young willows now their tender forms prostrate.

Wailing are the gales around my gullies,
As raindrops fall like mournful sheets of ice,
  While pure terror starts to chase
  Pain and suffering on my face,
For all the tended plants I can hear splice.

Now the morning dawns with trepidation,
And hearing all God's creatures breathe a sigh,
  I listen to the songbirds
  Trilling soft melodious words,
While last night's raging clouds now kiss the sky.

Lulu Gee

The Smile That I'd Die For

The last I saw my darling she was sitting on the train
Waving, blowing kisses, heading out for Bangor Maine.
She wiped the warm tear from her cheek and whispered, 'I love you,'
As I stood on the platform feeling though my life was through.

I waved a leadened arm, as the train made as to go.
It shook my little darling as she rocked two and fro,
The raindrops on my cheek were hiding tears upon my face
And I wondered if I'd ever meet my sweetheart in this place.

The train rolled out the platform and my love was on her way,
I watched it slowly disappear and I could only say,
Kiss me sweet my dearest darling, kiss me once again,
Then saw the smile I'd die for as I whispered her sweet name.

I'd carry that possession in the prison of my mind,
When life just gets too painful and becomes a daily grind.
I'll take out that sweet smile of hers and warm my deadened heart,
That smile that I would die for even though we had to part.

Dan Lake

Summer

Beyond the golden meadow
Warm buttercups amass
Where in between the clover
Our footsteps softly pass.
The heat of the midsummer
Makes every growing thing
Seek spirit for survival
With glints of wondering.

The burden of a heat wave
May make the meadow cry
As laughing rays of sunshine
Will be airless and dry
And skies aflamed will darken
For rain clouds to appear
Then cracks, rumbling will tell us
That thunders all too near.

Yet rainfall soft as kisses
Will once again replete,
The hidden life that's stirring,
So surely round our feet
And skies ablaze with splendour
Will make the shadows play,
Beyond the golden meadow,
Upon a summers day.

Lulu Gee

Rejection

I've taken some advice; I've tried again,
To win her I must take a different track.
I hope my ardour can withstand this rain
And doesn't get some more uncensored flack.
I know I must try harder that's a fact,
I hope she doesn't think me just a pain,
But after I've got off this verbal rack,
I'll carry on attempting my mountain.

To win her love and passion is my aim!
But feel I'm in a motorway tailback.
I want to get it right (to get acclaim),
To hear my wheels are purring soft click clack.
Instead I'm 'point to point,' riding bareback,
My dearest treats me with contempt, disdain,
I'll give my old sex drive a thorough whack,
I'll carry on attempting my mountain.

I think I have no reason to complain,
It's my fault that these boxes just won't stack,
I know my sweetie has no need to maim,
To beat me in some verbal base attack.
I've reason to believe, I might claw back
Some credibility I will regain,
For eagerness is something I don't lack,
I'll carry on attempting my mountain.

Envoi
My Lord, I must admit the past was black,
No more she sees me as that sad chilblain,
My guns are firing like a loud ack ack,
For I can see the peak of my mountain.

Dan Lake

Because of You

Because of you I wake each morn
And spring to meet the day,
To see the world in different hues
And hear the words you say.
I never get enough of you,
My old age I'll postpone,
For love I never thought I'd have,
For love I've never known.

Because of you my days reach out,
To share so many things,
Such as our love of poetry
And happiness it brings.
The touch of hands and lips that kiss
The smell of your cologne,
Such love I never thought I'd have,
Such love I've never known.

Because of you my nights are sweet
As honey from the bee,
As with the beauty of the night,
You pledge your love to me.
To see desire that's in your eyes
Reflecting in my own,
With love I never thought I'd have,
With love I've never known.

Lulu Gee

The Worst Encounter

She'd dabbled in mystical, touched the beyond;
Played with the Ouija board caressed the wand,
Enjoying the thrills that most mortals would dread
When notions of roguishness entered her head.

She'd buy the old house sitting high in the hills
And throw a wild party with cocaine and pills,
A chicken or two to be slaughtered and bled,
What an awesome idea, to awaken the dead.

The old house had lived through some barbarous years,
So legends abounded of hauntings and fears
Of ghosts that appeared in the rooms late at night,
It was said you'd go mad with the fear of the sight.

But she dressed the house in a shroud of cold gloom,
With candles and ancients and filled every room
With claymores and paintings that stared from the walls,
Encouraging demons to walk its dank halls.

The night soon arrived and she couldn't contain
Her glee as she watched lightning through the rain,.
The huge rolls of thunder that breached the night skies,
Reflected the madness in her foolish eyes.

The stream in the village was surging to flood
And villagers cowed with a chill in their blood,
They peered at the guests who unable to cross,
Turned back to go homeward regretting their loss.

She sat all alone in her sumptuous attire,
And listened to whispers that stemmed from the fire,
Beginning to doubt what she's tried to contrive
And watched the dark phantoms slow coming alive.

The coldness of hands as they suppressed her cries,
As death stared obscenely into her blue eyes,
It lifted her, danced her to waltzes by Strauss
For the Marquis De Sade had once lived in this house.

The Marquis de Sade had held in his cellar,
A lady of doubt by the name Rose Keller.
Used and abused by a man who's insane,
She escaped with her life from the torturous pain.

Our foolish young woman had woken the mind,
Of a monster of history cruel and unkind
And suffered the fate from beyond mortal breath,
In the hands of de Sade she had screamed for her death.

They found her bedraggled and bloodied at last,
The storm had abated but they were aghast,
At the state of her madness incurred all alone,
So never play games with the dark and unknown.

Dan Lake

Soon it shall be Spring

The north east wind is blowing still;
it's almost early spring,
when every poet finds his quill
and every bird his wing.
I long to kiss a sequined moon
to gently wish and slowly spoon.
  I long to kiss
  I long to kiss
and bathe where silver skies illume.

The north east wind is blowing still;
hoar frosts are all but gone
while crocus dance upon the hill,
no longer pale and wan.
I long to see springtime is here
to dream by waters crystal clear.
  I long to see
  I long to see
a love most tender, pure and dear.

The north east wind is blowing still,
as clouds unfold on high,
for this hour brings an icy chill
through veils of writhing sky.
I long to hear the young curlew
and pheasants in the tall bamboo.
  I long to hear
  I long to hear
my love betroth his love so true.

Lulu Gee

As I Look Upon You

Now the cool night is around me
I feel its misty veil,
Like wings upon a butterfly
As in the wind they flail.

Beneath the beauty of the night
I look toward the sky,
Where fireflies are whispering
And angels softly sigh.

I look upon you steadily
At peace in dreams and sleep,
While night shadows caress your face
I feel my love run deep.

We touch beneath the drifting moon
While wishing on a star,
That dreams we dream may be fulfilled
No matter where we are.

Then as the river meets the sea
To lap the darkened shore,
With kisses sweet we then avow
To love for evermore.

Lulu Gee

A Worn and Lonely Seat

She sat there now as she had done a thousand times or more,
Dreaming of a love who'd ever care.
The kitchen walls were closing in, she'd shut the open door,
Would he come and kiss her silver hair?
Hair once golden like her skin; she'd known a young girl's dreams,
Her knight, her Galahad would surely come,
But all she got was lust filled lies and now it all just seems,
She'd wasted life before it had begun.

She listened to the radio of songs from long ago,
Songs so filled with hope for times to come!
Now her tears were shed and the lyrics made her low
Where once they'd filled her with desire and fun.
These songs and all their words were firmly planted in her mind
But different now that love 'meant just a screw,'
No matter how she tried it seemed that love she couldn't find,
Her crumpled bed just left her feeling blue.

Where was her Galahad who would kiss each loving breath?
Fight the world to capture her sweet hand.
Her leeching liar had told her how he'd safeguard her from death
But all his words were written in the sand.
A smile from a stranger all at sea like passing ships,
A smile that she could hide down in her mind,
A lonely smile that asked for naught but played upon his lips,
A smile that said, 'hello' a smile consigned.

Should she seek the smiling stranger, would he prove like all the rest,
To be loathsome in the moments that they'd share.
Would he take her tired body and hold her to his chest,
Could he prove to be a man who'd dared to care?
Would he kiss her lips and make her feel that love was theirs to hold
And show her that her world could be complete,
Or was it just another dream that left her in the cold,
Ever crying on her worn and lonely seat.

Dan Lake

Am I the Woman?

Am I the woman,
To keep your heart racing
When northern skies quiver
With cold air that's bracing.
When witches on broomsticks
In darkness are chasing
The warlocks asunder
Their terrors emplacing.

Am I the woman,
Who when you are sleeping
Shall hold you close to me
To stop you from weeping.
When demons upon you
Are restless and leaping
And all through the night time
The spirits are creeping.

Am I the woman,
To wake in the morning
With kisses of passion
As daylight is dawning.
When nightmares have ended
And blue skies are warming,
While deep in the garden
Fresh flowers are forming.

Am I the woman,
Who when owls are flying
You'll hurry home to me
With love undenying.
At dusk cold and lonely
There'll be no more crying
For I am the woman
To love 'til you're dying.

Lulu Gee

The Blackthorn Tree

You'll find me in the hedgerows down the lanes where cowslips grow,
accompanied by hawthorn and my kin, the damson tree,
and while you look at bluebells growing wildly at my feet
you may, just as a fleeting glance, look up and notice me.

Around that time my petals of the purest white will form,
while whiskers like an old man's beard sprout from their yellow mouth,
but quickly as my blossoms fall, this 'mother of the wood'
falls silent to the eye to grow, my fruit that's facing south.

Those tiny green-like baubles swell beside my fearsome thorn
upon contorted branches bent and crooked, all askew,
but though I grow irregular, my wood is firm and strong
to bear my harvest of the gods for wise men to accrue.

October sees my wholesome yield, dark blue with angel dust,
the sprinkled wax that forms a bloom on every sour sloe.
For those with knowledge pick my plum not for a sweet dessert,
but make a jam or mix with gin to set the cheeks aglow.

Then as the year draws to a close, my leaves and fruits bestrewn,
another hunter casts his eye to find among my fare
a bough that's straight and strong of heart to make a walking stick,
but search he will and search he must to find that which is rare.

My powers are as strong today as they were long ago.
My bark, my leaf, my flowers sought to heal throughout the land,
this 'keeper of the secrets' this old friend of Wiccan charm,
so use, but don't abuse me or my thorn will prick your hand.

Dan Lake

My Winter Garden

Now that my garden is asleep
There's not so much I must upkeep,
Although some leaves are hanging still
And each night brings a frosty chill.

The beauty of the autumns gone,
Only the rose will linger on
As summer beds no longer cheer,
So pinks and reds will disappear.

The oriental poppy bows
As though these are her final vows,
I haven't seen a snail in weeks
A clustering in slimy cliques.

Last week the hostas said farewell
(Even surrounded by eggshell),
The snails had feasted at a pace,
So intricate, like antique lace.

Summer flowers, still heads aloft
Are now fatigued and brownly soft,
While breezes tremble trees so bare
Like spinning windmills in the air.

Around my door great spiders creep
In silken webs they spy and peep,
But now it's cold they'll come indoors
For Puss to torment with her claws!

And russets on the orchard floor,
A feast for badger's winter store,
Along with carrots and courgette
For when he ventures from his sett.

Nibbling mice have locked their door
To sleep tight curled on leaves and straw,
But squirrels still come down to see
The titbits I've put out for tea.

Now veils of rain will sweep the sky
And thunderstorms will surely cry,
So I shall put away my spade,
Until I hear spring's serenade.

Lulu Gee

I love to Fish

I love to fish and love this place
Where Pike and Perch ambush and chase,
Where Willows grow along the banks
And Water Voles take food with thanks.
I love to fish.

Fish I've dropped when cast in haste
When cast for Tench, large Roach or Dace,
And watched Kingfishers show me how,
To catch those fish, I should know now.
I love to fish.

Where Grebe swim with a funny face,
Industrious in their workplace
And gentle breeze blow bunny tails,
As silver birds leave vapour trails,
I love to fish.

Dan Lake

Afar and Beyond

Beyond my gated garden,
the road curves to the right,
it edges the horizon
where skylarks are in flight.
That's where my lover's waiting,
that's where he waits for me,
that's where one day I'll venture,
for all the world to see.

The burden that is winter
is barren as the tomb
and doesn't seem to worry
that I too need to bloom.
Perhaps when summer's splendour
looks down on Lammas land,
when roses scatter perfume
that's when he'll take my hand.

As apples start to ripen -
and fall about my feet
where hidden life is stirring
and bees make honey sweet.
Yet still beyond my garden,
I look to where he is
and hope before the Autumn
I'll feel his tender kiss.

Yet on the far horizon
more distant than my sight,
I know the moon is dancing
for his and my delight.
Perhaps he'll come in Autumn,
or will it be next Spring,
when I see a golden sky
with chaffinch on the wing.

Lulu Gee

Cold Tears

Today it won't stop raining but I shouldn't be complaining
For every drop of rain brings me to you.
God's tears upon my window remind me where the wind blows;
When we're apart my heart is always blue.

I look out on the heather and reflect this dismal weather
And in a way I'm happy to be sad,
For if the sun was shining I'd still ever be maligning,
Crying tears upon my old and worn keypad.

My day could be much brighter for this down at heart poor writer,
If the smile I dream of walked into my coil,
I dream of her so scented as we sit awhile contented,
Silently my world would slow uncoil.

My heart is always queasy and I know it's never easy,
As the cold tears chill my soul and never stops.
When she leaves me here so lonely I can think of her love only
And can't wait for her to come back from the shops.

Dan Lake

Margot's Shoes

Her tiny feet bled with the pain
From her last matinee,
A repertoire she knew so well,
She danced it every day.

En pointe her feet would pirouette,
Solo or pas de deaux,
In arabesque she looked divine
And I'm a connoisseur.

The spotlights loved her charisma
And her extending arms
Flowed like a willow in the breeze
Displaying all her charms.

Her glissades (gleesahds) made me skip a breath,
In floating pink chiffon
And in Giselle she stopped my heart,
As did her dying swan.

Her feet told many stories but
With each ballet performed,
She needed drugs to free the pain,
Of toes that were deformed.

With Nureyev she found new life
That lasted many years,
He said, their bodies danced as one,
And crossed many frontiers.

With each chasse across the stage
And jete (shuh-tay) that she flew,
Margot Fonteyn was magical
En pointe in lace tutu.

Her tiny feet bled with the pain
From her last matinee,
A repertoire she knew so well,
Until her dying day!

Lulu Gee

Sweet Amour

Those silk like thighs under that dress,
Those wanton eyes full of caress,
Those tender moments I possess
Fill me with hard desire.

You dance like Fontaine soft and slow,
You know I'm inflamed all aglow,
I shout to let the whole world know,
It's you who fans my fire.

You turn your head and show your face,
You drop your shoulder strap of lace,
Your tongue just gives your lips a taste
Of what is yet to come.

I'm mesmerised by your entrée,
You're naked as you slow display,
Those fabled lands where we can play
Among your moist kingdom.

Please let me burn my fire bright
And enjoy all your sweet delight,
As you allure and tease, invite
My rampant chanticleer.

Those lips that burn me to the core,
Those fingers excite me, implore,
To enter and make sweet amour,
Your cloistered soft pasture.

I dream of you, your sweet allure,
I am your slave, your paramour.

Dan Lake

A Day with You

As I sit and watch you fishing so contented and carefree,
I can see a little smile upon your lips,
when you think I am not looking I admire your dignity
and I feel my heart miss beats and do three flips.
There's a duck that gently waddles to the bank where I am sat,
he is beautiful from head to his wingtips
and as the sun beats down on me I reach for my new hat,
which I bought on one of my last shopping trips.
Now this place where you are fishing is bright eyed with life astir,
as I sit and listen to the bird song quips,
for today it is midsummer so I dream of wondrous things
and right now I'm dreaming of your soft warm lips.
The fountain in the distance sighs and shimmers pearly blue,
as a gentle breeze brushes my fingertips.
There are blossoms tempting butterflies and bees to rendezvous,
while sweet flirty little birds display courtships
and we laugh and tease like children as we eat our ice-cream treats,
mine is strawberry without the chocolate chips.
As the day is growing tired I can hear my own heartbeats,
as you take my hands in yours to kiss my lips.

Lulu Gee

Ego Vs Money

She knew I couldn't love her I'm a mercenary man,
Loving for reward not adulation,
She knew that she was beautiful and used to being desired
And confused at my awkward hesitation.

She whispered, 'do you like me' as we danced across the floor,
The warmth of her sweet body made me rise,
She felt my manhood fill with blood and dropped her hand to feel,
Softly she whispered passion in her eyes.

'Say you love me darling, that you will for evermore,
Say and all my pleasures will be yours,
State you can't live without me, is that too much to ask,
A word like dearest opens many doors.'

I wondered where her ego took her; this was just my job,
Everybody paid, she knew the rules,
She's beautiful, she's glamorous, she's everybody's dream,
But pay they must, from princesses to fools.

'You know this gun's for hire' I said, regardless of desire,
'You know I've always charged a little more,
You know that I can't fall in love; it's really bad for trade,
Let's face it I am just a male whore.'

Self obsessed and egotistic drove her on demanding,
I beg for her like other paramours,
She took me to her room and stripped, determined to succeed
And settled like a bitch there on all fours.

'Just say you love me big boy, then all this will be free,
Tell me you love me and it's yours,'
Then as she reached between her legs to show her moist warm prize'
She never heard me close her bedroom doors.

Dan Lake

Will You Love Me

Will you love me in the morning beyond the velvet sky,
when frost is lying on the ground and snow clouds wander by,
or on a sleepy afternoon when finches harvest fruit,
for their pretty newborn chicks in my old discarded boot.

Will you love me in a rainstorm that lasts the whole day long,
or out of tune I sing for you a silly ragtime song,
while yet again you cook for me with garlic and red wine,
with not a care for anything, not even my waistline!

Will you love me when I laugh with a tear here in my eye,
when your idiotic jokes make me catch my breath and sigh,
or when we dance beneath the moon that shimmers with delight,
or while we take a nightcap kissing tenderly goodnight.

Will you love me every springtime for all of evermore,
when the bluebells smell delicious upon the forest floor
and sycamores don every shade of green in every hue
and songbirds tell me once again that I'm in love with you.

Will you love me?

Lulu Gee

If I Could Write

If I could write the perfect words,
Contained within the perfect line,
That sets your mind to think again,
Embraced by love, encased by pain,
Enrapturing its sweet refrain,
So buried in its rhyme.

If I could write exquisite form,
That takes your breath and stills your heart,
To make you read and read once more
Each tiny vowel that you explore,
That you'd remember evermore;
A wondrous work of art.

But I am just a simple man
Who writes of love, or mystic birds,
Of summer's sweet or winter's snow
Or war and peace or skies that glow,
Who strives to gain that high plateau:
If I could write those words.

Dan Lake

Ask Not

Ask not how we shall love from now,
It's written in the stars
And in each lovely song we hear,
Strummed softly by guitars.
Nor ask me as I fall asleep,
If my heart is but true,
Because I'll have to tell you this,
I'll give my life for you.

Ask not if my heart beats as yours,
The moon should tell you so,
As will the fireflies in the trees,
Cast you a silv'ry glow.
And ask me not through veils of rain,
If kisses are like wine,
For when we kiss I tell the world,
That you, darling, are mine.

Ask not when strolling hand in hand,
Through poppies in a field,
If for eternity we'll love,
As wheat harvests will yield.
Nor ask when laughing at twilight,
As rainbows kiss the day
If I will stay as close to you
As you to me, I pray.

Ask not how we shall love from now,
We'll find a way, my dear ....somehow.

Lulu Gee

Red Riding Hood

Red Riding Hood full understood
The stories from her youth,
Told by mama in her boudoir
Of wolves that were uncouth.

Her path well-worn one early morn
Into the forest led,
Where vines entwined and were inclined
To cause fear where she tread.

Then in disguise to her surprise,
A wolf made himself known
And said a smile would help exile
The spell from an old crone.

Just one small kiss won't go amiss
So with much haste and speed,
She kissed his nose and with repose
Hoped soon he would be freed.

'Twas then she saw without a flaw
Nor yet even a trace
Of wolf to harm, but with a charm
He looked into her face.

His body bare he was aware,
Her breaths of mortal sighs,
Enflamed desire to light his fire,
In his now human eyes.

With gentleness and warm caress,
He kissed her silken lips
And loved her there in his warm lair,
Just where the hollow dips.

She cried aloud and softly soughed
And from her tears he sipped,
Then stroked her flesh in half darkness,
As sun with moon eclipsed.

Red Riding Hood misunderstood
The stories from her youth,
Told by mama in her boudoir
Of wolves that were uncouth!!!

Lulu Gee

Dolly Daydream

My Dolly with her brown eyes sweet
And dainty ballerina feet,
Affectionate, with heart of gold,
I'm sure God surely lost the mould.

I found her on a rainy day,
As trucks drove fast and sent their spray,
On to this little dog so lost
And frozen in the morning's frost.

Her coat wriggled and squirmed with fleas,
As I bent low upon my knees,
To scoop her up into my arms,
To be enraptured by her charms.

My house she found so warm she stayed
And in two years she's never strayed,
Instead she's become my best friend
Assured with me she can depend.

It was two years ago this spring,
This little dog pulled my heart string.
When I was low she brought me love,
Sent by an angel from above.

The first time she sat on my knee
I felt the need for poetry
So with a pen I wrote a line
And suddenly the world was mine.

Lulu Gee

Cogito ergo sum

I think therefore I am, is that the truth?
I was, therefore I cogitate the now.
Reflecting on the content of my youth,
a time that commonsense should disallow.

Much of what is past is fabricated,
a politician redefines his quill,
the wonders of those years accentuated,
while burying the truth on old Boot Hill.

I think therefore I am that seems amiss,
I doubt therefore I think, seems right to me,
the past is past and just would be remiss
to think too much, or would you disagree?

I doubt therefore I am, therefore I think
and wonder if I am the missing link.

Dan Lake

Thimble

Now Thimble is I have been told
Not very young nor very old,
You'll think me rash and quite absurd
But Thimble thinks she is a bird.
Each day she flies with pied wagtails
Over the hills and through the vales,
While oak trees talk above her head,
'Just give her time,' is all they said.

The willow tits, sparrows and crow,
Along with chaffinch seem to know
That Thimble thinks she is a bird
But no-one seems to say a word.
The eiders with their fluffy down
And sparrows with their feathers brown,
Built her a nest of woven hair
As soft as cashmere, I declare!

Down where the river gently stirs
Beneath the singing conifers,
Where here the birds gather to rest
And Thimble comes at their request.
The goldfinch, dunnock and cuckoo
Along with waxwings rendezvous,
When bats take flight to dart and skim
And sunlight starts to tremble dim.

There in the midst is Thimble, sweet
With little hands and little feet,
Sitting upon soft scented grass
As owls and moths go drifting past.
Her fairy wings she tightly furls,
As fast asleep she gently curls
And in the quiet and the hush,
Sweet lullabies are sung by thrush.

Lulu Gee

Lulu Gee

Lulu Gee lives in the south of England by the river Wey.

She worked in finance until she retired and now writes

her lovely poetry full-time with her two dogs Teddy and

Dolly never far from her side.

In 'The First Encore,' a collaboration with her friend

Dan Lake we are spoilt with a vast selection from their

repertoires to enjoy, not least of course their favourite topic, love

(with plenty of kisses!)

Her two previous books have done extremely well and she

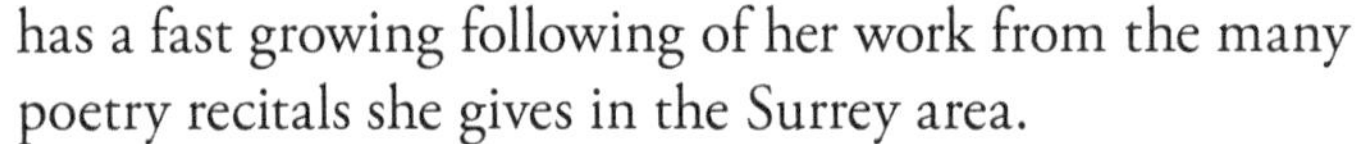

has a fast growing following of her work from the many poetry recitals she gives in the Surrey area.

At present she is working on a collection of fantasy poetry that will appeal to children, especially her new character Twizzy Mouse.

This new collection just one year on from her first with Dan Lake which was entitled 'I Won't Sing if You Won't Dance' is a 'must have' for all of Lulu's fans and for anyone who enjoys beautifully crafted poetry.

Dan Lake

Dan Lake lives in Hempstead in the Medway Towns and was born and raised in Kent in the UK. He has travelled and collected an eclectic group of friends from wherever he has been, giving him a wonderful understanding of the differences in human nature and mankind in general.

Although a gregarious person, underneath lies a quiet and reserved spirit which when touched upon allows his pen to write some very romantic poetry as you will read here. His poetry also abounds with joy and humour, but also war and pain and has a desire to write about life in general reflecting the people he has met.

His colourful life allows him to reach out to the reader who instinctively understands where his mind is set in each individually crafted piece, so immediately making a connection with Dan himself. Those of you who have read his first compilation of poems in the book 'I Won't Sing if You Won't Dance' written in collaboration with Lulu Gee will already know that he is a fine poet.

Those that haven't, simply enjoy…

www.ingramcontent.com/pod-product-compliance
Ingram Content Group UK Ltd.
Pitfield, Milton Keynes, MK11 3LW, UK
UKHW041947190726
13854UKWH00004B/1846

9 781449 086428